From
Entrepreneur
to
Infopreneur

From
Entrepreneur
to
Infopreneur

Make Money with Books, eBooks, and Information Products

STEPHANIE CHANDLER

John Wiley & Sons, Inc.

Published by John Wiley & Sons, Inc., Hoboken, New Jersey.
Published simultaneously in Canada.

For general information on our other products and services or for technical support, please contact our Customer Care Department within the United States at (800) 762-2974, outside the United States at (317) 572-3993 or fax (317) 572-4002.

Wiley also publishes its books in a variety of electronic formats. Some content that appears in print may not be available in electronic books. For more information about Wiley products, visit our web site at www.wiley.com.

Library of Congress Cataloging-in-Publication Data:

Chandler, Stephanie, 1972–
   From entrepreneur to infopreneur: make money with books, ebooks, and information products / Stephanie Chandler.
      p.   cm.
   Includes bibliographical references.
   ISBN-13: 978-0-470-05086-6 (pbk.)
   ISBN-10: 0-470-05086-1 (pbk.)
   1. Information services industry—Management. 2. Information resources—Marketing. 3. New business enterprises—Management. 4. Small business—Management. I. Title: Infopreneur: make money with books, ebooks, and information products. II. Title: Make money with books, ebooks, and information products. III. Title.
   HD9999.I492C457   2007
   381'.45002068—dc22

                                                                                        2006007863

Printed in the United States of America.

10   9   8   7   6   5   4   3   2

CONTENTS

CHAPTER 4

CHAPTER 5

CHAPTER 6

CHAPTER 7

CHAPTER 8

CHAPTER 9

CHAPTER 10

PREFACE

I'm a great believer in luck, and I find the harder I work, the more I have of it.
—THOMAS JEFFERSON

Thousands of business owners have already discovered the secret to selling information via books, eBooks, special reports, teleseminars, audio recordings, workbooks, and other information products. Some use these products to add revenue streams to their existing businesses, while others earn the bulk of their income from their info products.

I noticed this trend and began to wonder if there was really money to be made from selling information. Then I realized that not only was I interested in becoming an information provider, but that I was already part of the customer base.

I have invested thousands of dollars in books, eBooks, audio recordings, seminars, classes, and workshops over the years. I love this stuff! I seek out smart people to teach me something because if I'm not learning something new, quite frankly, I get bored. I'm still out there investing in information products at every turn, supporting business owners that I admire, and eagerly seeking information.

I've learned a lot by consuming information. Not only have I read hundreds of books, but participating in teleseminars and workshops has been an invaluable tool in helping me grow my businesses. Not every product investment has met my expectations. Truly successful infopreneurs are the ones who provide value and make consumers want to return for more. The rest may make a first sale, but if they don't deliver, customers won't return. Then they must work twice as hard to make their information businesses profitable.

My own journey into becoming an infopreneur began by accident. In 2003, I kissed off corporate America and opened Book Lovers Bookstore in Sacramento, California. The challenge of starting a new business was invigorating and the process led me to discover a new passion: helping other entrepreneurs find the same freedom that I did. I wanted others to know that there could be life after corporate America so I began writing my first book,

The Business Startup Checklist and Planning Guide: Seize Your Entrepreneurial Dreams!

Long before the book was published, I realized that I needed a strategy for reaching my target audience. So I sketched out a rough business plan and launched a content-rich web site: BusinessInfoGuide.com. The mission of the site is to provide lots of free resources to entrepreneurs. I compiled business start-up resources for industries ranging from cleaning services and event planning to public speaking and virtual assistance. I learned about search engine optimization and Internet marketing and started publishing a monthly newsletter. Before I knew it, my site traffic and subscriber base were exploding.

Eight months after the site launched, the book was ready to meet its audience. Thanks to my prepublication promotion efforts through the site and e-zine, I started receiving preorders a full two months before the book was available. By the time it was ready, sales were occurring naturally with what felt like very little effort.

I knew I wanted to expand my knowledge transfer beyond books and began investigating how to sell eBooks, teleseminars, and other information products. Naturally, I looked for books to help me accomplish my goals. But I couldn't find a single book out there that told me everything I needed. There were a few good books about self-publishing, a handful of poorly written eBook guides, plenty of marketing books, but nothing that brought all the information together. There wasn't a single book that painted the whole picture or discussed the plethora of information product opportunities.

So in the same way I planned to start my first business (the bookstore), I began planning my infopreneur business. I interviewed existing infopreneurs. I studied web sites. I ordered eBooks, signed up for teleconferences, and purchased audio collections. I compared the quality of each and made note of what I liked and didn't like, what worked and didn't work. Before I knew it, I had a new book idea that I knew I had to write.

I also began to test what I had learned. I started by listing some special reports for sale on my web site. I was both shocked and thrilled when my first sale happened just days after the first products went live. I have continued to develop new products and maintain my legacy products. Not only are there financial rewards, but I love receiving messages from customers who have benefited from my products. Product sales occur with minimal effort while I sleep.

I have also developed products that I can sell at the back of the room when I speak. I sell workbooks, tips booklets, and CDs of teleseminar recordings. I believe that success comes from pricing my products fairly and making sure they are loaded with value. My goal is always to exceed my customers' expectations, and this strategy has served me well in every business endeavor.

A lot of really intelligent people are out there making money by sharing what they know. There are also some people who are taking advantage of consumers by skyrocketing their prices and providing minimal value. As with any business, we all have a choice when it comes to conducting ourselves with integrity. If you're reading this book, I urge you to be one of the "good" infopreneurs. Not only will you sleep better at night, but your business will inevitably flourish.

Each chapter of this book concludes with the story of a successful infopreneur. These smart and resourceful business owners figured out how to profit from what they know—and do so with integrity. These people are successful because they have each developed a formula for delivering quality information and generating repeat business. If you study their business models, you are sure to discover a world of opportunity all your own.

There is an eager market of buyers out there. My goal is to show you how to develop and market your own products. One of the greatest advantages of selling information products is that they can essentially become passive income—money you make while you sleep. Once the work is done and you've created a high-quality product, and you've automated the product sales and delivery process, your primary role will be to continue marketing your products. That's where the real fun begins.

There is no single secret to success, though there are many tips to help you along the way. You'll learn them as you read along, but here are some basics:

- ✔ **Everyone is an expert at something:** Whatever your expertise, whether it's fly fishing, yoga, parenting, knitting, sales, or customer service, you have something to teach others who know less than you do.
- ✔ **The Internet is a powerful venue for reaching customers:** Learn to maximize your reach in order to run an efficient and profitable business.

✔ **Marketing is an *investment* in your business:** Rare is the business that succeeds without marketing. Try a variety of strategies and repeat the ones that work best.

✔ **Don't be afraid to ask questions:** Nobody has all the answers and most people are willing to help. Just ask!

✔ **Invest in other people's information products:** Not only will you have the chance to learn something new, but you can evaluate the content and begin to understand the formula for success. It's also good karma to support people whose work you admire.

✔ **Persevere:** This is my favorite word in the English language. There will be days when you feel as if you are spinning your wheels for nothing. But eventually, with enough effort, something magical happens. It all starts to come together.

✔ **Never stop learning:** I don't care what industry you are in. Things change. Rules change. People change. Stay on top of your area of expertise. Learn about new technology. Remember how much fun it can be to learn something new and how rewarding it is to succeed.

For months, I have been fielding questions from family and friends: "What is your new book about?" I watch as some of their eyes glaze over—especially those who don't spend a lot of time on the Internet. "It's about becoming an infopreneur," I tell them. "I'm going to show people how to make money selling eBooks and information products." The ones who own businesses—or want to be entrepreneurs—perk up. The rest of them look at me as if my face is melting.

Whether you want to start an infopreneur business or expand your existing business by selling information products, this book is here to help you. My hope is that I've made it easy for you to navigate through the business of selling information. More important, I want you to be inspired.

Get out your highlighter and sticky notes. Take notes as you read. Open your mind to new ideas and learn from the examples provided. And when you've launched your infopreneur business, drop me a line and tell me about it. My suspicion is that the information business is about to explode, and I can't wait to ride that wave with you.

Information Product Opportunities: Fire Up Those Revenue Streams

Small opportunities are often the beginning of great enterprises.
—DEMOSTHENES

The term *infopreneur* is a relatively new industry buzz word that is making waves because it opens doors for entrepreneurs to generate new streams of income. Simply put, an infopreneur sells information. Information products are offered in many formats:

- ✔ Books
- ✔ eBooks
- ✔ Special reports
- ✔ Audio products
- ✔ Videos
- ✔ Teleseminars and web seminars
- ✔ In-person seminars/workshops
- ✔ Workbooks

✔ Tips booklets

✔ Virtually any format in which you can deliver information

Selling information can create new revenue streams for an existing business, or lay the foundation for a new business opportunity. Many successful business owners have been doing this for years. Here are some examples:

Tom Antion (www.antion.com) is the author of *The Ultimate Guide to Electronic Marketing for Small Business,* as well as numerous other books and dozens of information products including:

✔ Audio CDs and cassettes for $19.95 to $49.95

✔ Books, both self-published and contracted with major publishing houses

✔ eBooks for $9.95 to $97.00

✔ Seminars starting at $265.00 per attendee

Tom promotes his products online and through speaking engagements. He also proudly admits to making millions from his products.

Joan Stewart is a publicity expert and founder of wwwpublicityhound .com. Joan currently offers over 100 information products including:

✔ Tips booklets for $5.00 each

✔ Special reports for $10.00 each

✔ Recordings of teleconferences on CD for $39.95

✔ Subscription to her bimonthly newsletter for $39.95

Joan promotes her business with a free weekly newsletter and through speaking engagements.

Dottie Walters is the author of *Speak and Grow Rich* and is the founder of www.speakandgrowrich.com. In addition to published books, Dottie sells:

✔ Recordings of her audio seminars for $35.00 to $125.00

✔ Subscriptions to *Sharing Ideas* (a magazine for professional speakers; a two-year subscription costs $95.00)

✔ Videotaped programs for $69.00

✔ Workshops and seminars from $395.00 to $1,995.00

Dottie promotes her business through speaking engagements and networking within the professional speaking industry.

Dan Poynter is the author of *The Self-Publishing Manual* and numerous other books, and is the founder of www.parapublishing.com. Dan has built an enterprise based on his expertise in several topics: self-publishing, parachuting, serving as an expert witness, and cats (that's right, cats!). Dan publishes a popular free e-zine with a subscriber base of over 25,000 people and sells the following products through his web site:

✔ Special reports for $4.00 to $19.95

✔ Mailing lists for $3.00 to $107.00

✔ Power packs that combine all his products for $297.00 to $897.00 Dan conducts dozens of speaking engagements each year and even sells attendance to a popular weekend workshop that he hosts in his own home.

Throughout this book, you will learn about these and other successful infopreneurs—savvy business owners who either run their entire businesses by selling their information products, or use their products to reel in additional revenue. Their stories appear in interview format so you can read their actual words and find out how each has managed to build and grow an information product business. Some happened by accident, and some were carefully calculated. All have achieved admirable success.

BENEFITS OF INFORMATION PRODUCTS

Revenue is often considered the primary benefit to information products. While money is a big motivator, there are numerous advantages you may not have considered.

PASSIVE INCOME

Perhaps one of the most compelling reasons to sell information products is the opportunity to generate passive income. Passive income is money that is generated without extensive ongoing effort by the business owner. Rental property income is the most traditional example of passive income. Once an information product is created and the distribution is automated, sales can occur with little additional effort.

Cost of Entry

The cost of creating electronic books and special reports is minimal. If you already have a computer and word processing program, the biggest investment is likely to be your time. You may want to invest in a PDF creator program, though you can still generate products without one.

Expert Status

Publishing a book enhances your credibility and can lead to speaking engagements and media interviews. Many authors treat their books like fancy business cards, using them to open doors of opportunity. With the right spin on your topic, media exposure could bring you a windfall of new business. Just look at any author who has made it onto the *Today Show* or the *Oprah Winfrey Show.* Even an article in a local newspaper can prompt dozens of readers to buy your products or visit your web site.

New Products Bring New Customers

As you add more info products to your line, you spin a web of opportunity. Each product may appeal to each customer differently. Some may buy one product, others may buy another product, and ideally, most customers will return and purchase multiple products.

Marketing Opportunities

Each new product helps you reach new markets with your advertising efforts. You automatically create a new reason to send a press release when you announce a new product. You can also promote the new product to your newsletter subscribers and to other businesses that complement yours. These targeted marketing opportunities could change with each new product introduced since each could appeal to a different audience.

CROSS-PROMOTION OPPORTUNITIES

Giveaways are a fantastic use for info products. You could reward new subscribers to your e-zine by giving away a free eBook or special report. Or you could send your downloadable product to other business owners and allow them to distribute it for free, provided they include your author bio and a link to your web site. This strategy will attract new customers as well as increase exposure to your target audience.

POTENTIAL FOR CORPORATE DEALS

You can negotiate rights to resell your content. Paulette Ensign, founder of www.tipsbooklets.com, sells her tips booklets by the thousands to businesses that reproduce them as giveaways for their own customers and employees. Not only does she make money selling the reprint rights to the booklets, but she reaches thousands of potential new customers. You can create a similar opportunity with any of your info products. You could resell your books, audio programs, or workbooks to corporations or other professional organizations to give away to their employees, sales staff, or customers, or for use as training materials.

WORD OF MOUTH

Getting new business by word of mouth is one of the best kinds of advertising that money cannot buy. Companies like Yahoo!, Craigslist, eBay, and Half.com were built into huge operations thanks in large part to the buzz generated by enthusiastic site visitors. When you create premium products with tremendous value, inevitably your customers are going to talk about it. The challenge is to make your products buzzworthy. If you can exceed your customers' expectations, the buzz will happen naturally and over time your revenues will grow as a result.

GENERATING INFORMATION PRODUCT IDEAS

Everybody is an expert at something. If you run a successful business, that makes you an expert in your industry. If you have a passion for a hobby, sport, or other special skill, you can use what you know about the topic to educate others. Here are some ways to generate product ideas:

- ✔ Consider what information you have that other people want to know about.

- ✔ Survey your customers and ask them what they would like to learn.

- ✔ Make a list of your skills and interests. Identify topics that you can elaborate on and that would appeal to an audience of buyers.

- ✔ Teach people how to do something—You could explain how to do what you do for a living, how to create something, how to market your type of business, or how to locate resources.

- ✔ Create a directory. Do you have a list of 50 or more resources that people in your industry need? Sell it!

- ✔ Take a broad topic and develop a niche. John Gray, author of *Men Are from Mars, Women Are from Venus* capitalizes on relationship advice. Following the success of his first book, he went on to write *Mars and Venus on a Date, Mars and Venus in the Bedroom,* and even *The Mars and Venus Diet and Exercise Solution.* In addition to carving out a niche and creating multiple products, Gray used savvy marketing strategies with his title and branded his books with the memorable "Mars and Venus" theme.

- ✔ Read books about your field of interest. Is there a book that covers an important piece of information in one chapter that deserves to be expanded? Could you write a whole book or special report about that topic?

- ✔ Jump on a trend. This book is a great example of an emerging industry trend since becoming an infopreneur is a hot topic in the small business community. There are dozens of books that cover portions of the topics discussed in this book; however, this is the first book to bring it all together. Find a trend in your industry and develop products that the market is hungry for.

- ✔ Get dialed in by hosting teleseminars. For topics, think about the valuable information you can provide in a one-hour call. Better yet, make a list of potential guests that you can interview. You could charge for attendance at the seminars or offer them for free and sell the recordings. Joan Stewart, founder of www.publicityhound.com, has mastered the art of earning income from her teleseminars by interviewing popular guests and charging for both attendance and recordings after the fact.

✔ Take your show on the road. What could you teach a live audience? Outline some topics and consider teaching at your local adult learning center or becoming a professional speaker and host your own workshops. You can also sell recordings of your live presentations. Mark Victor Hansen, cocreator of the popular *Chicken Soup for the Soul* series of books and numerous other books and products, hosts seminars throughout the year. Admission to his Build Your Mega Speaking Empire workshop costs $995.00. Not only does he make a mint in registration fees, but you can be sure he sells plenty of books and add-on products to attendees.

✔ Create an interesting visual presentation. A videotape or DVD of a demonstration, speech, or technique can be sold to eager buyers. These can be especially effective for crafts, food, the fitness industry, and other hobbies.

✔ Take an inventory of the people you know and see if you can incorporate them into your projects. People like real-world examples and advice from experts. Consider interviewing your peers and include excerpts in your print publications.

Table 1.1 lists some information products for various businesses.

KEYS TO SUCCESS WITH INFORMATION PRODUCTS

To convince customers to get out the credit card and buy from you, your product strategy should include the following elements:

✔ **Quality:** There are a lot of information products out there, and some are downright lousy. Make sure that whatever you produce is of the highest quality. Written documents, audiotapes, and video programs should all be professionally edited.

✔ **Expertise:** Demonstrate any credentials that you have in your field. This is not the time to be shy. Publicize your education, experience, awards, or achievements in the area that is your specialty.

Type of Business	Potential Info Products
Professional speaker	Directory of resources such as speaking venues Subscription to your newsletter Workbook Book that covers your topic in-depth Audio recordings of presentations Video recordings of presentations
Chef or restaurant	Recipe collections (with themes like quick meals, pasta, healthy options, appetizers, party foods) Cooking tips Video demonstrations Cooking classes
Jeweler	Explanation of how jewelry is rated Resources for buying and selling estate jewelry Resources for buying or selling online How to repair or restore jewelry at home
Pet services	Pet first aid Recipes for pet treats Tips for caring for an aging pet Training techniques for dogs, cats, ferrets, and others How-to start a pet business
Financial services company	Retirement planning advice Property, stock, bonds, or other investment advice How to buy with no money down How to clean up a credit report How to get certified as a loan agent
Musician	How to play an instrument How to perform a special style of music How to book paying gigs Tips for breaking into the business
Comic bookstore	How to identify collectible comics How to publish your own comics Resources for comic collectors Price guides Subscription newsletter
Hobby or craft	How-to guide Directory of resources for selling products Tips for marketing this type of business Workshops or classes

TABLE 1.1   How to develop information products for different types of businesses.

Strangers are not going to buy from you unless you can demonstrate your expertise and ability to deliver on your promises.

✔ **Value:** There is a fine balance when determining the price of products, and too many infopreneurs price their products out of the ballpark. Check to see how your competitors are pricing their products. Some set their price points higher to demonstrate the extreme value of the information they are selling. If you use this pricing strategy, be sure you are delivering information that is worth the hefty price tag.

✔ **Delivery:** Product delivery needs to be efficient and timely. Customers who purchase electronic products such as eBooks and reports want instant gratification. Though you can manually e-mail electronic products once you have completed a sale, this strategy will make you a slave to your online business. Ideally, you should set up a system to automate the delivery process. Added advantages of automation are that you won't have to constantly check e-mail for sales notifications and you can make money and deliver products from anywhere in the world.

✔ **Marketing:** Few businesses can survive without marketing. You need to let people know you are there so you can entice them into buying from you. A solid marketing plan is essential to success with info products.

✔ **Repetition:** This is part of marketing, but warrants its own line item (a repetition in itself) because it is so critical. The average consumer needs to be exposed to a product *six to eight times* before making a buying decision. This means that you need to expose your audience to your product offerings and your business over and over and over again. You can do this with your web site, e-zine, speaking engagements, articles, and other publicity efforts.

✔ **Development:** All info products should be up to date. At the same time, new products should be in development and complement the other products you have available. Think about how McDonald's structures its business. The fast-food chain relies on a group of staple products (Big Macs, fries, Quarter Pounders) and introduces new products throughout the year. To test market viability, some products are only available for a limited time. The products that sell best are added to the permanent menu. New products also attract new customers who may, in turn, purchase some of the legacy products.

STRATEGIES FOR PROMOTING INFORMATION PRODUCTS

Much of this book is devoted to marketing: It is important to think about this factor before you even get started as an infopreneur. If you're going to sell info products, you will need a strategy to promote them. Consider the following tools:

- ✔ Build a web site specializing in topics related to your products. Provide free information as a teaser or sample of what you have to offer. If you offer free information that is useful, you may eventually convert many of those free users into real buyers.

- ✔ Find public speaking engagements (including workshops, seminars, and classes). If you speak at an adult learning center, your bio—with your name—is distributed to everyone who receives the catalog, even if the class only seats 15 people. Seminar-speaking experience also helps you earn credibility while gaining valuable exposure.

- ✔ Free teleconferences can help get the word out if you take advantage of advertising with your online networks. Ask peers to announce your events in their e-zines or on their web sites. Although you aren't selling your product up front and instead are providing information, you are exposing people to your name and your products.

- ✔ Newsletters and e-zines are an inexpensive yet valuable way to market to your customers. Make it easy for web site visitors to subscribe, and then send out consistent and valuable content on a weekly or monthly basis.

- ✔ Up-sell and promote additional products when someone makes a purchase by including a brochure about your other products or by offering a special discount on a related product at the time of purchase.

✔ Establish yourself as an expert in your field by being seen and heard everywhere. Participate in interviews, publish articles in print and online, and seize every possible opportunity to get your name out in the world. Brand yourself as an expert.

✔ Take advantage of media exposure. Radio is an inexpensive way to reach a lot of people in a short amount of time. Many talk radio programs interview experts through a call-in format. If your topic is interesting enough to reach a broad range of listeners, you could go on a radio tour right from the comfort of your own home. Print publicity is also beneficial. Find news angles for your topic and contact newspaper, magazine, and TV reporters.

✔ Create an affiliate program. Offer other businesses the opportunity to sell your products and pay them a percentage of each sale.

✔ Swap advertising with web sites and e-zines that reach your target market.

TRY THIS

Make a list of potential topics and products that you want to create. Ideally, you will develop a long list of opportunities. Once you make your list, prioritize which ideas you want to tackle first. It can be overwhelming to take on too much at once, so determine where your best opportunities are (in the sales world, we call this "low-hanging fruit") and begin the product development process.

Infopreneur Profile

Joan Stewart
The Publicity Hound
Port Washington, Wisconsin
www.publicityhound.com

PRODUCTS:

- Forty-nine five-page special reports with titles too numerous to mention ($10.00 each)
- CD recordings of teleconferences ($39.95 each)

- Cassette recordings of teleconferences ($14.97 each)
- Printed transcripts of teleconferences ($10.00 each)
- Subscription to bimonthly newsletter ($49.95)
- Mentor program ($1,500 for six months, $2,500 for a year)

Brief Description of Contents:

The title is an inch wide and content is a mile deep. In other words, very narrow specialized topic with in-depth information.

Who is your target audience for your materials?
Anyone who wants to self-promote.

Where do you sell your materials?
Through my web site, e-zine, blog, and affiliates.

When did you first publish your material?
About five years ago.

What made you decide to publish electronic reports?
It's much easier and cheaper than hard copies.

How does your publication enhance your business?
It positions me as an expert. It brings in a lot of revenue. And my web site sells while I'm sleeping.

What was the process you used to publish?
For special reports, I simply bought a special report on how to create special reports, written by Jeffrey Lant, an information entrepreneur. Actually, each special report was originally intended to be a chapter in a hard-copy book. I thought I'd write a special report that would become chapter one of my book and sell it at my web site and through my e-zine; then when I had 20 reports completed, I'd start looking for a publisher. They sold so well, so quickly, and in such volume, that I would have been crazy to turn them into a book that I couldn't have sold for much more than $25.00. Now, I have 49 reports.

How do you market your materials?

I market primarily by excerpting tips for my weekly e-zine. If people like and need the tips, they buy the full report. This works like a charm.

What has been the most challenging part of the publishing process?

Keeping so many reports in front of people on my list continuously.

What has been the most rewarding part of the publishing process?

The revenue.

What have you learned from the experience that you would like to share with others?

Don't offer special reports in hard copy, like I did originally, or you'll find yourself in front of your printer all day. Offer electronic versions only.

Looking back, is there anything you would do differently?

I would have never offered print versions. And I wouldn't have hesitated to raise the price like I did. I was reluctant to raise the price from $7.00 to $9.00. When I finally did, I saw no drop in sales.

CHAPTER 2

Celebrity Sells: Achieving Expert Status

Believe one who has proved it. Believe an expert.
—VIRGIL, *AENEID*

B ecoming a recognized expert in your field is crucial to success as an infopreneur. People like to learn from experts because expertise equates to credibility. Would you want parenting advice from someone who doesn't have children? Would you take a kayaking class from someone who has never been out on the open water? Would you board a plane that was being flown by someone who didn't have a pilot's license?

Not only does expertise give you credibility with your customers, but the media love experts. Pick up any newspaper or magazine and read the articles. Almost every article has a quote from an expert—an industry professional, a doctor, an author, or a business owner. The media actually seek out experts. Table 2.1 lists some names you already know, thanks to the media.

What do all these experts have in common? The most obvious is that each has written a book—or several books. Just being an expert is the beginning: The next step is telling the world about it, and one of the quickest ways to do that is to become an author.

Expert	Expertise
Dr. Phil McGraw	General psychological issues
John Gray	Relationships (*Mars and Venus* series of books)
Tom Hopkins	Big business, corporate America
Robert Kiyosaki	Finances, real estate, money
Donald Trump	Real estate
Martha Stewart	Decorating, homemaking
Rachel Ray	Cooking, food
Suze Orman	Personal finances
Stephen Covey	Success
Deepak Chopra	Spirituality

TABLE 2.1   Well-Known Experts

No matter whether publishing is part of your game plan, people believe in experts. And once you announce your expertise to the world, it can be easier to sell your products and services—even if you never plan to write a book.

Plenty of Internet superstars have never published a book. And there are just as many experts right in your backyard. Your neighborhood dry cleaner is an expert at stain removal, even though he's probably never written a book about it. Wouldn't you believe his advice on tackling tough stains? Give him a copy of this book! He could create a whole new stream of revenue from his expertise.

THE ANATOMY OF AN EXPERT

Experts come in all varieties with varying levels of education and experience. Most experts have the following qualifications:

- ✔ **Education:** Doctors and those with advanced degrees earn their expert status through education. If you have a degree in your subject matter, you've already won half the battle.
- ✔ **Talent:** You don't always need years of education to become an expert in your field. Martha Stewart began her career on Wall Street, yet she has created a billion-dollar enterprise based on her creative talent. There are just as many experts who have earned their wings by capitalizing on their passion.

✔ **Experience:** If you have spent the past five years working in customer service and have developed a passion and understanding for that field, then you have enough experience to call yourself a customer service expert. Experience in virtually any industry, hobby, or activity can make you an expert.

✔ **Ownership:** Simply proclaiming yourself an expert and owning that title is enough to get started. Once you believe it, others will follow. If you want your expertise to work for you, you have to learn to toot your own horn.

✔ **Confidence:** Experts believe in their knowledge. Would you want a surgeon to operate on you if he seemed nervous about performing the procedure? Heck no! Though nobody has all the answers to a given subject, as long as you have most of the answers, you are well on your way. Remember *The Little Engine That Could*? You can accomplish anything if you believe in yourself.

✔ **Growth:** Savvy experts stay on top of their industry by continuing the learning process. To stay abreast of industry news, you should study the trends, read trade publications and books, join trade associations, and participate in industry-related activities. The more you know, the more your confidence will increase and the more value you can provide your customers.

BUILDING AN EXPERT PLATFORM

Once you have established your expertise, the next step is to tell the world about it. As mentioned, writing a book is one of the quickest ways to get started. But it's not the only way. The following strategies will help you build your expert platform.

CONSULTING

If consulting isn't already part of your repertoire, perhaps it should be. Becoming a consultant in your field instantly boosts your expert status. In addition to elevating your expert platform, you can potentially generate significant income from your services.

There are many ways to go about implementing consulting services. You can offer one-on-one consulting services for fees ranging from $50 to $500 or more per hour. Some experts find that by elevating their fees, they may limit the number of people they work with, but they also create a perception that their time is extremely valuable (thus elevating their expert status even further).

You could also dedicate a certain amount of time to a mentoring program for clients each month. This program might include teleseminars or e-mail coaching for your clients. Or you could dedicate several hours per month in individual or group training time.

Before announcing your consulting services, make sure you plan out your approach. You will need to develop a contractual agreement for clients and outline the services you are willing to perform. Consider what services your potential clients will need. Better yet, survey your target audience to evaluate what kind of services you should offer. Don't forget to check out your competition and the services it is offering. Spend some time developing your plan and soon your earnings potential could increase dramatically along with your expert status.

ESTABLISH A WEB SITE

There is no easier way to reach a worldwide audience than to establish a presence on the Internet. Web sites are relatively inexpensive to maintain and can reach an audience around the globe. For more information on the importance of a web site and how to build yours, see Chapter 8.

Once you have a web site up and running, you should begin building a database of visitors. Publishing your own newsletter or e-zine allows you to create ongoing communications with your fans and promote your products and services. More details on this smart marketing strategy can be found in Chapter 9.

PUBLIC SPEAKING

Giving talks and lectures is an excellent way to reach a broad audience. Keynote speakers with celebrity status can command speaking fees upward of $10,000. Even if you speak for a lesser fee or no fee at all, giving presentations gets your name out in the world and creates opportunities for selling products. Public speakers are in demand for all kinds of events. Here are some potential venues:

- ✔ Large corporations
- ✔ Trade shows and conferences
- ✔ Colleges and schools
- ✔ Businesses (e.g., a financial planning office could bring in a real estate expert to give a seminar for its customers)
- ✔ Libraries
- ✔ Community centers

Not only does speaking enhance your credibility and status, but it gives you an outlet for lucrative back-of-the-room sales. All kinds of information products can be sold at the back of the room including books, tips booklets, audio and video programs, and workbooks. If you are serious about becoming an infopreneur, public speaking is an excellent way to grow your business.

To build your skills as an engaging speaker, consider joining Toastmasters (www.toastmasters.org). They have chapters all over the United States where fellow speakers meet and refine their speaking skills. Also make sure you list yourself as an available speaker with any trade organizations that you belong to. Many keep lists of speakers for referral when someone calls to inquire about a presentation. You might also want to consider joining a speaker's association such as the National Speakers Association (www.nsaspeaker.org) or Professional Speakers Association (www.professionalspeakers.org).

Tips for Successful Presentations

If the mere thought of standing up in front of an audience makes your knees quiver, you should know that you're not alone. Public speaking is one of the top fears listed by Americans and for good reason—most of us don't do it very often. My personal theory is that it stems from the fear of failure.

After spending several years as a technical instructor and in sales, speaking to audiences of all sizes, I've built an arsenal of strategies for presentations. The truth is, even the most seasoned public speakers get at least a little nervous before they step onstage. But the seasoned pros also know the tricks to delivering seamless and engaging presentations.

Keys to Writing a Winning Presentation

✔ **Create an outline:** You may not think you need to outline your topic, but it will likely save you time in the long run. Outlining your entire presentation before you start to write it lets you organize the flow of information and ensures that you have included all the relevant topics.

✔ **Determine the proper number of slides:** If you are using Power-Point, the rule of thumb is that each slide will require two to three minutes of discussion. If you are speaking for an hour, 60+ slides will be too many. You know your topic best, but 25 to 30 slides would probably be appropriate for a one-hour presentation.

✔ **Limit the amount of text:** Slides that are too wordy will cause your audience to lose interest faster than the freeway fills up at rush hour. Try to stick to no more than five bullet points and whenever possible, show instead of tell. This means that you should illustrate your topic with charts, graphs, graphic images, or other visual representations to keep your content engaging.

✔ **Minimize the bells and whistles:** A lot of activity or noise on your slides is bound to distract your audience. Resist the temptation to pepper your slides with flashy animation or music unless it truly enhances your message.

✔ **Proofread and check spelling—twice:** Nothing kills a presentation faster than grammatical mistakes. You could be the most engaging speaker in the world, but spelling errors and misplaced punctuation can cause your audience to lose focus and question your credibility. I once watched an executive give a presentation with an emphasis on aspirin. He spelled aspirin incorrectly on a series of slides, and half the room was talking about it by the time the presentation was over, which caused them to miss much of an interesting discussion. If you don't trust your own proofreading ability, have a colleague review your presentation.

Keys to Presentation Delivery

✔ **Practice, practice, practice:** If you don't have an audience to test your materials on, lock yourself in an empty room and start talking to the chairs. It may seem awkward at first, but it's the best way to calm your nerves and to be thoroughly prepared. If you've practiced to the point of practically memorizing the whole speech, you will launch into autopilot and deliver a flawless performance when showtime arrives and stage fright kicks in—even if your brain checks out.

✔ **Pace yourself:** Nervous presenters often talk too fast and rush through the material. When you practice your speech, time it and give yourself some room for questions or interruptions. To help with pacing, consciously pause between sentences and slides. Two seconds may feel like an eternity to you, but it allows your audience time to absorb what you've just said. Even taking a slow, deep breath between sentences and slides can slow you down and calm your nerves.

✔ **Record your performance:** Professional speaking programs use video cameras to show students how to improve their presence on stage. As painful as it may be to watch yourself on film, this is the best way to discover your flaws and nervous ticks. You may find that you sway, play with your pen, jingle the change in your pocket or look like you're dancing because you're moving around so much. Using a video camera to capture your performance lets you identify your nervous habits and break them before you leave the audience talking about how many times you said "Um."

✔ **Use note cards or cheat sheets:** Even the president uses a teleprompter when giving his speeches, and you have the right to use notes or 3 × 5 cards to keep you on track. Just be careful not to read them or rely on them too heavily; if you've practiced, this shouldn't be a problem. Avoid writing your entire speech verbatim on the cards since they will be difficult to glance at and could cause you to end up reading from them. Instead, write down only short bullets to jog your memory and keep your flow.

✔ **Warm up the audience:** The best way to get the crowd on your side is to open with humor. Start with a joke or quip that is related to your topic. For help with locating material, check out www.the-jokes.com or www.jokes.com. Both offer free access to all kinds of one-liners.

✔ **Keep an eye on the clock:** Audiences and event organizers appreciate speakers who stick to the time line. Keep an eye on the time so you can speed up or slow down. You can also ask someone in the audience to give you hand signals if necessary. If your presentation ends before the allotted time, open the floor to questions.

✔ **Talk to foreheads:** Make an effort to speak to the whole audience, which means looking around the room and making each attendee feel as though you are speaking directly to that person. If eye contact makes you even more nervous, then talk to foreheads. Nobody will notice your lack of true connection, yet you will still convey your ability to engage the entire room.

✔ **Don't forget to smile:** Use inflection in your voice and keep a smile on your face. Your audience will mirror your behavior and if you get onstage with a stone-faced, monotone delivery, the whole audience will be bored (or asleep) by the time you're done. Weave in some humor or anecdotes and let your personality shine through.

Whether you're speaking to a room of six people or six hundred, these tips should help you become a more polished presenter. Remember that the number one key to success is to be as prepared as possible. Another great way to learn new techniques is to critique the performance of other presenters. Watch presentations on television or at venues in your area. Notice how the speakers engage the audience and watch for tricks that you can incorporate into your own regimen.

TEACH CLASSES

Expand your public speaking platform by teaching classes. Expert instructors are in high demand with local adult learning centers, colleges, and even businesses. Classes can range from one or three hours to a semester. The schools will even pay you for being an instructor, and most will allow you to sell your products in the back of the room. Check out the local education centers in your area to inquire about teaching in your field of expertise. Also check out one of the largest adult education centers in the country: www.learningannex.com.

ADDITIONAL RESOURCES

- ✔ SpeakerNetNews is a newsletter for people in the speaking profession: http://speakernetnews.com
- ✔ Speaker Match links speakers with events: www.speakermatch .com
- ✔ World Class Speakers and Entertainers offers a directory of public speaking professionals: www.speak.com
- ✔ BusinessInfoGuide has a directory of resources for the public speaking industry: www.businessinfoguide.com/speaking.htm
- ✔ *Speak and Grow Rich* by Dottie Walters
- ✔ *Never Be Boring Again* by Doug Stevenson

PUBLISH ARTICLES

You can reach a broad audience by getting articles published in magazines and newspapers or across the Internet. Many publications will print a short author biography (known as a *byline*) with your article where you can mention your web site link. This valuable exposure not only gets your name out in the world, but brings new web site traffic from readers who like what you have to say.

C. Hope Clark, the founder of the popular web site FundsForWriters .com, says, "Writing articles is the best method to promote my work. Whether I receive payment for them or not, the simple publication of my expert words about grants, markets, and other funding streams motivates readers to learn more and purchase my eBooks and trade paperbacks online. Articles act as a little sample of what to expect in the books—they are the best sales tool I have."

Clark says her subscriber base has grown exponentially as a result of publishing articles, and my own experience has been identical. Each time one of my articles comes out, even in a small publication, I watch my subscriber list grow and my book sales spike.

Many print publications will pay you for your efforts ranging from $0.20 to $2.00 per word; although just as many will only compensate you with a byline. Trade magazines are an excellent place to start since they are often in need of writers. Consumer magazines can also be a source for your articles, although breaking into the popular magazines on the checkout stands at grocery stores is extremely difficult. It is best to start with smaller or regional publications.

Depending on your expertise, you can develop all kinds of slants for article topics. For example, a career coach could write articles about job hunting, effective interview skills, negotiating salaries, and dressing for success. These articles could appeal to business magazines, regional magazines, or even general interest publications.

You can check the masthead of any publication to locate editorial contact information. Most publications have a web presence, and many list writer's guidelines that tell you what types of articles the magazine is looking for and how to submit them.

Editorial calendars can also be helpful since they list each issue's focus for the upcoming year. It is always a good idea to note if you are submitting an article that would be a good fit for a theme in the editorial calendar. Often the editorial calendar is listed in the advertising section of the web site so advertisers know what's coming up.

There is also an annual book called *Writer's Market* by Kathryn S. Brogan and Robert Lee Brewer. This hefty volume lists hundreds of publications, their rules for submission, and whom to contact. The online version is available at www.writersmarket.com, and for a nominal subscription fee, you can have instant access to hundreds of editorial contacts at magazines and newspapers.

Every publication has a different policy regarding rights to print articles. Some magazines only publish articles that have not previously been printed elsewhere. In that case, you are offering the magazine first serial rights. The magazine may ask for exclusive rights for a period of time, such as 30 days. A few magazines ask for "all rights" which means you cannot publish the article elsewhere ever again. If a magazine requests all rights from you, make sure it is worth your effort. You want to be able to reuse most of your articles and only want to give away rights if the publication reach is extremely broad.

Many smaller magazines and newspapers don't care much when or where the article has been published previously. The publication may still opt to purchase reprint rights and may even offer you a nominal payment of $10 to $100.

Once you have written an article and have reread it several times to correct any errors, add your byline to the bottom of the copy. Your bio should look something like this:

Edna Entrepreneur is a career coach in Dayton, Ohio, and is the author of *The Career Planning Book*. Visit her web site at www.xxxxx.com.

If you are submitting by e-mail, your message should look something like this:

Article Submission
"Ten Sizzling Ways to Boost Online Sales"
By Stephanie Chandler
875 words
[article text]
About the Author:
Stephanie Chandler is the author of *The Business Startup Checklist and Planning Guide: Seize Your Entrepreneurial Dreams!* and founder of BusinessInfoGuide.com, a directory of resources for entrepreneurs.

Dear [editor's name],
You are welcome to reprint this article provided the author bio is included. Thank you very much for your consideration.

To view a sample of my published articles, please visit www .StephanieChandler.com. (Don't worry about this line if you don't have any previously published articles. Just be sure to add it to your correspondence once you have some published articles to your credit.)

Best regards,
Stephanie Chandler
[contact information]

Some editors will notify you if they decide to print your article, though some of the smaller publications won't bother since you offered the rights along with your submission. Some may contact you to confirm where to send a payment and will request your Social Security number since they are required to report payments at tax time.

I often submit articles only to discover months later that one has appeared in a magazine because a reader sends me a message about it. This is a great marketing strategy so I never mind when this happens. Since I include my mailing address when I submit, occasionally a publication will be kind enough to send me a copy of the magazine in which the article appears—but don't expect this to happen often.

Some of the larger magazines will not even consider article submissions and instead require a writer to submit a query letter first stating your intention to write an article for the publication, outlining the topic, and explaining your qualifications (expertise) for writing it. If you want to write for a magazine that follows this protocol, use these guidelines to write your query:

- ✔ Use your letterhead if you have it.
- ✔ Make sure to write a professional business letter and include your contact information.
- ✔ Address the letter to a specific person. Avoid using "Dear Editor" for a salutation as most recipients find it offensive.
- ✔ Open with a description of the subject and explain why it is important. Be concise and give enough detail to make it convincing, without being too wordy.
- ✔ Explain your credentials.
- ✔ Most queries should be kept to one page.
- ✔ If you have written articles for other publications, include two or three photocopies with your submission. In the publishing world, these are called "clips."

Here is a sample query letter:

Dear Ms. Jones,
When job hunting, many women need help with writing an effective resume. There are key elements in writing a resume that many forget to employ. A resume should be:

- Chronological
- Written without spelling or punctuation errors

- Tailored to the position for which the person is applying
- Proofread by several people

I am a professional career coach and I have written a 1,000-word article called "Resumes that Rock" that I would like to submit for your consideration. I hope you will agree that the readers of *Women in the Workforce* magazine will find this article useful.

I am also the author of *The Career Planning Book* and have published articles in a variety of publications including *Career Journal, Job City Times,* and *Job Hunter's Weekly.*

Thank you for your time. I look forward to hearing from you.

Best regards,
Edna Entrepreneur

Don't overlook web sites that also accept article submissions. Many web sites operate on a limited budget and appreciate articles written by experts. Locate web sites that relate to your area of expertise and search for writer's guidelines. If no guidelines are provided, contact the site owner or editor and ask if she accepts articles. Attach an example for her review.

There are also several free content sites that allow you to post articles that others can reprint in their newsletters or e-zines. Articles posted on these sites can proliferate across the Internet and end up in all kinds of web sites and newsletters. You won't receive any payment for these, but it is an excellent strategy for building your name recognition.

The following web sites accept article submissions on a wide variety of subjects:

- ✔ www.ideamarketers.com
- ✔ www.ezinearticles.com
- ✔ www.articlecity.com
- ✔ www.amazines.com

⚡ HOT TIP ⚡

If you write articles and distribute them as free content, add a page on your own web site to promote them. A "Free Content" page maximizes the distribution of your expert articles. Include your author bio and state, "These articles may be reprinted provided the author bio is included."

Branding

You can gain a lot of mileage by coming up with a catchy title or phrase that captures the essence of your expertise. Several of the infopreneurs profiled in this book have built brand recognition for themselves:

✔ Romanus Wolter is the "Kick Start Guy."

✔ Joan Stewart is the "Publicity Hound."

✔ Dan Poynter is the "Father of Self-Publishing."

✔ Joe Vitale is "Mr. Fire."

Developing a brand for yourself makes you memorable to your audience and provides another method to convey your expertise. If you decide to use this strategy, be sure to include your phrase in everything you do: your web site, marketing materials, presentations, e-mail signature, bio, business cards, and everywhere else. The key to success with branding is to make your tag line synonymous with your name.

Blogging for Dollars

A web log, also known as a *blog,* functions like an online diary. The popularity of blogs has exploded in the new millennium, generating new fodder for watercooler chats. From columnists and business owners to students and political activists, blogs have opened doors of opportunity for sharing information and attracting customers.

There has been much controversy over the use of blogs to promote online businesses. In early stages of the technology, Internet search engines were prioritizing key words in blogs and listing them with higher priority in search results. Since then, the rules have changed, and continue to change, but one thing is certain; people are talking about blogs.

If you have something interesting to share with the online community, a blog is an excellent method for doing so. Blog publishers have complete control over their own content. Many business owners use blogs as an extension of their business promotion. In the same way that online forums and articles reach potential new customers, a blog can help you discover a new audience and showcase your expertise.

Many bloggers post to their web log daily, although since you own the content, it's up to you how often you post a new message. You could post every other day or even once per week. You could also share a blog with a business associate or invite contributors and divide the workload.

Hosting a blog is free or low cost through a variety of providers. Blogs can be listed in the public directory of the blog hosting provider, making it easier for new readers to find you. If you are interested in starting your own blog, or want to peruse some existing blogs, check out these providers:

✔ www.blogger.com

✔ www.livejournal.com

✔ www.tripod.lycos.com

ONLINE EXPERTS

An online venue that allows you to promote your expertise is www .AllExperts.com. This web site lists hundreds of subjects from sports and arts to business and automotives, and it allows site visitors to ask questions of the volunteer experts.

You must complete a simple application and wait for approval to become a volunteer expert. Once approved, you can create a profile that lists details about you and your business. You will then receive messages from site visitors through e-mail sent by AllExperts and you can respond using its online form. Perhaps the best advantage is that your responses are archived on the site and can show up in Internet searches for years to come. Be sure to include a thorough e-mail signature at the end of each posting you submit.

This service allows you to gain exposure all over the world, although it can also be time consuming. I have found several benefits to acting as a small business expert on this site. Not only has it attracted new web site visitors and book buyers, but the questions I receive reflect current trends in the industry and show me what's on the mind of new entrepreneurs. I have the system set to send me no more than two questions per day so my time investment is minimal and I still find that the benefits outweigh the time it takes to participate.

There are several other services that allow you to list yourself as an expert for a fee. One popular source used by journalists is www.profnet.com. You can also perform an Internet search for "experts" and will receive dozens of directory listings.

MAXIMIZING MEDIA EXPOSURE

One of the most effective methods for promotion is media exposure that typically begins with a simple press release. Newspapers, magazines, radio stations, and television news shows rely on press releases to locate news and human interest stories. Anyone can send a press release, but to get the attention of reporters, it must be professional, newsworthy, and appealing to a broad audience.

A press release should be brief—one or two pages max—yet include enough details that a reporter could write a short article based solely on the information provided. The release should also have an enticing "hook." The trick is to make the hook interesting enough to capture the interest of the reader.

REASONS FOR SENDING A PRESS RELEASE

The mere fact that you or your company exists is usually not a good enough reason to send a press release. Remember, the media's goal is to tell the public a story, not to advertise your business. Your release should never sound like a sales brochure for your business. If you want to receive media coverage, you have to create a story.

Here are 10 ways to make your press release newsworthy:

1. Relate your business to an upcoming holiday or anniversary.
2. Describe a new product or service that solves a consumer problem.
3. Reveal results of a survey you have taken.
4. Announce a contest or winners of a contest.

5. Announce awards or recognition you have received.

6. Announce charitable or fund-raising activities.

7. Announce events you are hosting.

8. Take a controversial position on a hot topic.

9. Share details of a strategic partnership or alliance you have formed.

10. Offer something for free—product, service, demonstration, event, and so on.

CRAFTING YOUR RELEASE

Follow these guidelines to write a press release that gets the attention you want:

✔ Read sample press releases before writing yours so you understand the proper format. Some good sources for locating professional releases are www.businesswire.com and www.prnewswire.com.

✔ Start with a proper heading that includes your contact information. When listing phone numbers, indicate a day and evening number (reporters may call at odd hours) or simply list your cell phone number.

✔ Give the release an enticing title that captures the reader's interest and print it in **bold** type.

✔ Double-space the body of your release for easy reading.

✔ The first paragraph should summarize the content by including the basics of who, what, where, when, and why. You want to lay the foundation and include your hook immediately with engaging copy that prompts a response from the media.

✔ As awkward as it may be, it may be appropriate to quote yourself and write the release as if someone else has written it for you.

✔ Do not let grammar or spelling mistakes sneak into a press release. Make sure you edit your writing thoroughly and have a friend—or better yet two friends—review it for errors and content.

There are numerous services that you can pay to distribute your release to hundreds or thousands of markets. One of the most popular online services is PRWeb (www.prweb.com). PRWeb charges from $30 to $80+ to increase the distribution of your release. Some other services to consider are www.ereleases.com, www.free-press-release.com, and www.xpresspress.com. It is also a good idea to send the release out directly to appropriate publications. You should maintain your own media list and send the release out accordingly.

Before you send your release, be sure you are prepared to answer interview questions. You may receive calls from reporters within a few hours of sending your release and will want to have thoughtful responses ready. Consider writing a list of points you want to make and keep it handy.

A press release can be worth its weight in gold because a news story usually generates more buzz than any form of paid advertising. Don't be discouraged if your first attempt doesn't receive the attention you want, simply try again until you find the formula and pitch that works:

Press Release Outline

FOR IMMEDIATE RELEASE

Business Name
Address
Contact Person
Phone
e-mail

CATCHY HEADLINE INDICATED IN BOLD CAPITAL LETTERS

Date—City, State—Lead paragraph including summary of who, what, where, when, and why.

Body of the press release should include three to six paragraphs. Include quotes from yourself or others (make sure to get their permission). Write the content as if it were an article you were reading in a magazine. Don't forget to double-space the text.

Paragraph Two
Paragraph Three
Paragraph Four
Paragraph Five

About the company: Include a brief overview of the company such as the date founded and the mission of the business.

How to Contact the Media Directly

I have sent out hundreds of press releases over the years. Though they can pay off and hit the media lottery, I've also had just as much success, possibly more, by contacting editors and reporters directly.

Media people are incredibly accessible because they rely on the public to provide them with stories. The contact information for reporters can often be found at the end of an article or on a publication's web site. Editors are also listed on web sites.

You can write an e-mail to a reporter or editor anytime. One strategy you can use is to compliment a reporter on a story he wrote or tie a story in with your business or product. For example, Joe Reporter publishes an article in *Newsweek* about the dangers of day care centers. If you are a child care expert, you can write to Joe and let him know that you have 10 tips for keeping kids safe or that you are available as an expert source if he decides to write a follow-up article.

When I opened my bookstore in Sacramento, California, I wrote to the reporter for the *Sacramento Bee* whom, I noticed, had written several features on area businesses. I introduced myself, told the story of how I had left corporate America to open the bookstore, and offered to discuss my story with her if she was interested. Before I knew it, I received front section coverage, including several photos and an article so flattering, I couldn't have written it better myself!

Another strategy is simply to introduce yourself as a source. If you are an expert in relationships, you can contact editors and reporters who cover this topic and let them know that you are available if they need a source for a future story. Be friendly, brief, and include a link to your press kit (see Chapter 9 for information on how to create your press kit).

Although it can be time consuming to seek out reporters or editors one at a time, the results can make it worth your while. You never know when your timing might be perfect because the reporter was planning to write a story about your industry. And even if he doesn't want to write a story about you now, you might hear from him in three, six, or even twelve months after you make contact. Each time you send a message, you have planted a seed. Some will grow, some won't. But you'll never know unless you try. Be sure to add each contact to your own media database so you can access the information when you need it again.

PUBLICISTS AND PUBLICITY LEADS

If you have a budget for publicity, hiring a publicist can bring you plenty of media exposure. Publicists work with their clients to help achieve publicity goals. Since most publicists charge several hundred dollars per hour and work on a retainer basis, this is not always an affordable option for everyone.

Pay for placement is a relatively new concept where you, the expert, pay a publicity service when it books you with a media outlet (television, radio, or print PR opportunity). Annie Jennings (www.anniejenningspr.com) has a firm that specializes in pay for placement for experts. You complete a profile and get on a mailing list to receive announcements for new media placement opportunities in your general subject area. When an opportunity arises that interests you, you contact the firm and let it know. The firm then decides if you're qualified—several people may be competing for the opportunity. You agree to pay a fee (typically several hundred dollars) if the service connects you with a media professional.

Another option is PR Leads (www.prleads.com). Described as the "Expert Resource Network," PR Leads is a subscription service ($99.00 per month) that sends its subscribers media leads by e-mail. A message might indicate that a reporter who is working on an article for *Newsweek* about small business cash flow needs quotes from a finance expert. It's up to the subscriber to follow up on the lead in a timely manner in order to be the first and most qualified expert to respond.

For radio publicity, Radio TV Interview Report (www.rtir.com) is a print publication that is distributed to radio and television producers. The company sells half- and full-page print ads in the publication. Most of the advertisers are authors. One of the greatest advantages of radio publicity is that in most cases, you can conduct interviews from your own home or office.

NURTURING MEDIA RELATIONSHIPS

Once you make contact with someone in the media, whether an editor, a producer, or a reporter, be sure to nurture the relationship. Send a thank-you note after you receive any kind of coverage. This seems like an obvious action to me, but most people don't take the time to do it. Not only can you show your genuine appreciation, but you give the reporter a reason to re-member you. You never know when the reporter might have another story where you could serve as an expert source.

Many folks in the media are not allowed to accept gifts. This is espe-cially true of newspaper professionals. You may want to show your apprecia-tion with a basket of cookies or a bottle of wine, but it could get the reporter in trouble. Instead, stick with a thank-you note.

The most difficult challenge is establishing an ongoing relationship. One way to do this is to continue reading a reporter's articles, and when one is particularly appealing, send a quick note of kudos. And if you run across an interesting story idea, even if it has nothing to do with you or your business, forward it to the reporter. Gestures like these will endear you to this busy professional and build a relationship that can last for years.

PREPARING FOR MEDIA APPEARANCES

If you're invited to speak on a radio or television show, you will want to be fully prepared for the adventure. Guests who impress get invited back, so be sure to dazzle them at every step.

TELEVISION

Most national programs will ask you to send a video recording of a previous media interview. If you don't have one, start by contacting your local news stations to conduct interviews and build your media experience. Even a five-minute interview on your local news program can be enough to send to the big guys.

Many television shows, such as the *Today Show* or *Oprah,* screen guests before inviting them to appear on the show. A producer interviews them and evaluates their ability to appeal to an audience. Producers will note how ar-ticulate you are, how well you answer questions, and how smoothly you per-form under pressure. Make sure you are fully prepared to speak to the media before you make your first pitch by anticipating questions and outlining your answers ahead of time.

If you are invited to be a guest on a television show, use these tips to make sure you are prepared:

✔ Send a copy of your book (if you have one) to the producer prior to the show. You may want to include several copies for the staff, too. They will be more likely to help promote a book they have read and enjoyed.

✔ Provide the producer with a list of questions you are prepared to answer. She may not use them, but then again, she might.

✔ Provide the producer with a graphic image of your book (if you have one) and your web site address. Your goal is to get her to put these up on the screen during your interview.

✔ Check in with the producer a couple of days prior to your appearance to reconfirm your time slot and answer any last-minute questions she may have for you.

✔ If you are an out of towner, schedule your arrival for the day before your appearance. Airport delays can be disastrous and you don't ever want to be the guest who didn't show up.

✔ Make sure you bring the contact information for the producer with you in case of emergencies.

✔ Arrive at the studio early.

✔ Avoid wearing patterns or prints. Solid colors look best on camera, especially in shades of blue. Break out your best suit or business attire. It is better to be overdressed than underdressed.

✔ Both men and women should wear face powder to prevent glare.

✔ Women should consider hiring a professional makeup artist the morning of the event.

✔ Be an engaging and energetic guest. Smile, use inflection in your voice, and try to look comfortable.

✔ Avoid looking at the camera. Instead, focus on the host and occasionally, the audience.

✔ Don't speak over the host. Let her lead the interview her way, even if you don't really like the way she's handling it. Remember, it's her gig and you are the *guest*.

✔ Use anecdotes to illustrate points and inject appropriate humor.

✔ Avoid using industry jargon or terms that the general public won't understand.

✔ Don't pitch your book or your business. Let the show do that for you.

✔ Bring a VHS tape with you and ask for a recording of your interview.

✔ Remember to write thank-you notes to the producer and host following your appearance.

RADIO

One of the greatest advantages of radio exposure is that many interviews can be conducted from the comfort of your home or office. This type of virtual tour can allow you to perform dozens or even hundreds of appearances without ever setting foot on an airplane.

However, visiting the studio can also have advantages. An in-person appearance allows you to get to know the host, producer and support staff. This could result in a longer than expected interview or the host may help pitch your products simply because he or she likes you. If you can leave a lasting impression, you will be more likely to be invited back in the future.

Many of the tips listed for television can be helpful with radio interviews. Here are some additional suggestions for calling in from home:

✔ Disable call waiting or cancel the service altogether. You probably won't miss it.

✔ Use a high-quality corded phone (land line).

✔ Make sure you have a quiet place to conduct the call.

✔ Keep children and pets contained for the duration of the interview.

✔ Silence your cell phone.

✔ Keep a glass of water handy. Avoid carbonated beverages as they can make you gassy.

TIPS FOR MAKING THE MOST OF YOUR INTERVIEW TIME

✔ Ask the producer if you can offer giveaways to callers. For example, you could give away several copies of your book or tips sheet. You could make it even more fun by asking callers to answer a question or participate in a quiz.

✔ Bring along a list of tips such as "Top Ten Ways to Make More Money" or "Twelve Solutions for Managing a Busy Household." If a break is coming up, suggest that listeners get a pen ready to write down the "hot tips" you're going to share with them after the break. That way, they will also have a pen handy when you mention your web site, book title, or other contact information.

✔ If the host forgets to mention your web site, work it into the conversation when you're wrapping up the show. For example, "Thank you, Joe, for having me here today. If listeners would like to reach me, visit my web site at www. . . ."

✔ Make a special offer for listeners. For example, set up a page on your web site where radio listeners can receive a discount on your products, services, or books. Let the audience know that you are making the offer available just to them "today only."

✔ Ask the producer to list your web site address and 800-number (if you have one) on the station's web site.

✔ Ask the producer for a recording of the interview.

✔ Remember to thank everyone involved after the interview has ended.

🔥 HOT TIP 🔥

If you need some part-time assistance managing administrative tasks for your business, hiring a virtual assistant (VA) could be the answer. Virtual assistants are independent contractors who work remotely (usually from their homes) and provide administrative services such as writing business letters, managing a database, developing marketing copy, and managing web site content. Most VAs are hired on retainer for a set number of hours each month or on a per project basis. To locate a VA, visit the member directory from the International Virtual Assistants Association: www.ivaa.org.

Infopreneur Profile

Dottie Walters
Walters International Speakers Bureau
Glendora, California
www.speakandgrowrich.com

PRODUCTS:

- *Sharing Ideas* (magazine for professional speakers), now in its 26th year of publication, $95.00 for a two-year subscription which includes our International Directory of Agents and Bureaus
- *Never Underestimate the Selling Power of a Woman* (paperback, Willshire Book Co., $7.00)
- *Speak and Grow Rich* (paperback, Prentice-Hall Press, $17.00)
- Audio albums ($39.95 to $125.00)
- Speak and Grow Rich Master Weekend Seminar (held at Dottie's home, $599.00)
- Consulting (two hours for $400.00)

Who is your target audience for your materials?
Speakers' bureaus, speakers, authors, and everyone connected to the world of paid professional speaking.

Where do you sell your materials (your own web site, online directories, Amazon, etc.)?
All of these, plus we have a catalog of our products, and we frequently sell out of products at my speaking engagements and seminars. We also take many telephone and mail orders here in our office. We take pride in sending out our orders the day we receive them.

What made you decide to self-publish?
Most of the things I have self-published were audio programs. Sometimes I have combined a book with an audio program. My latest album and book is titled *Learn to Find, Please, and Keep Commercial Sponsors*. It has been very popular.

How does your publication enhance your business?

Sharing Ideas is very popular. I love the journalistic opportunity. My background has been in that field. In high school I was advertising manager and feature editor of our Alhambra High School *Moor.* I later worked on the *Los Angeles Times Daily* newspaper in its advertising department, and I also started and ran for 10 years a competitor to "Welcome Wagon." We covered most of Southern California.

Sharing Ideas has provided an avenue to promote not only our business, but also our subscribers. We publish information that is on the leading edge in the speaking community.

What is the process you use to publish?

I put together a file for each book so that I can slip in ideas from magazines or the newspaper or an idea that came to me at my desk, or even things that arrive in my mailbox. I fasten a note to each item and tag the file for the chapters of my book. When one section gets full, I start the actual writing on my computer.

How do you market your materials?

For my Master Seminar Weekend, we include an attractive bag filled with my materials for each attendee. The cost is included in the seminar registration fee. We also have a back-of-room materials table where our audience can come up and buy any number of our products, or a bag which contains many of them at a special price. We also use back-of-room sales for our out-of-town seminars. The Internet has been a real success for selling our products and seminars.

What has been the most challenging part of the publishing process?

Proofing. You need [to have] a great speller doing it, and you yourself must do it, too, for content.

What has been the most rewarding part of the publishing process?

Last week we had a booth at the NSA [National Speakers' Association] Convention held in Atlanta. We had an attractive lighted display, featuring my book *Speak and Grow Rich* in the center of it. Literally hundreds of speakers came by and stopped to say hello to me and to tell me that my book had been the book that showed them the way for their careers. I was so glad to hear them say so. They had not only bought my book, they had used it and benefited from it! I was so touched I went through a box of Kleenex!

What have you learned from the experience that you would like to share with others?

In all of my seminars, speeches, and classes, I tell the story of how I began with cardboard in my shoes pushing our two babies in a dilapidated baby stroller built for one. I had no college education; my father had abandoned my mother and me as I was [about] to enter high school. However, I found jobs at many different businesses all through high school and learned about customer service, being a good (or bad) boss, and much, much more from every job I worked at during that period.

I love to read about the lives of people of achievement. One of Albert Einstein's quotes helped me a lot. He wrote, "The Solution is always located at hand." I borrowed my neighbor's typewriter and she gave me a wonderful gift, a whole ream of typing paper.

My sweetheart had returned from the South Pacific battles—he was a staff sergeant in the marine corps and was gone four years. We were married and bought a little tract house and a dry-cleaning franchise (he had been in that business before the war), and God gave us two beautiful children, a boy and a girl. Then there was the recession. No one was buying dry cleaning. I asked my husband Bob if I could write a "Shoppers Column" as I had done in high school. He was so discouraged he could not answer me.

I did write the column and things began to turn around. The "Solution" *is* at hand. You have to find it.

Looking back, is there anything you would do differently?

I am so grateful for the help God gave me in every part of my business, my speaking career, and in the books and other products I have created with His constant help. I had no idea when I started that Shopper's Column, that I would speak in many countries around the world, appear on hundreds of radio and TV shows, and be featured in many, many magazines not only in the [United States] but worldwide.

Author Aspirations: Effective Writing for Books

The best way to become acquainted with a subject is to write a book about it.

—BENJAMIN DISRAELI

S tudies show that as many as 80 percent of Americans want to write a book. Wow! That's a mind-numbing number of potential books. But the reality is that most people don't have the time or the true determination to realize their author aspirations. It is no secret that it takes a lot of work to write a book, and for some it may just be a pipe dream—something they plan to tackle when they retire and have more free time.

Others realize that publishing a book can equate to a lucrative business opportunity and public recognition. In this case, it's not just a hobby, it's a job. Nonfiction books are always in demand. People crave information, and the best books stay in print for many years.

RainToday.com released a survey in 2006 called, "The Business Impact of Writing a Book." Of the 200 business book authors surveyed, a whopping 97 percent reported that publishing a book affected their business practice either positively (49 percent) or extremely positively (47 percent). Other advantages of publishing were cited in the report:

- ✔ 75 percent of respondents reported a strong or very strong influence in generating more speaking engagements.
- ✔ 63 percent of respondents reported a strong or very strong influence in generating more clients.
- ✔ 53 percent of respondents reported a strong or very strong influence in charging higher fees for services.
- ✔ Every single author (100 percent) reported that publishing a book generated more publicity.

The report also included comments from many of the authors surveyed. Bob Bly, author of *The White Paper Marketing Handbook* said, "It established me as a guru in my field." Ford Harding, author of *Rain Making: The Professional's Guide to Attracting More Clients* said, "Publishing books has been very advantageous in networking and meeting new people. If I'm interested in talking to someone and I send them my book, the chances of me getting to meet with them are much greater than if I wasn't an author."

Alan Weiss, author of *Million Dollar Consulting* said of publishing, "It created an entire second career for me, which was consulting to consulting firms and consultants. . . . It's one of the two or three most important things I have ever done to market myself."

NO TIME TO WRITE?

If you can't imagine how you would ever find the time to write a whole book, then I have some great news for you. *It's not as hard as you think.* A typical book consists of a minimum of 60,000 words. This sounds like a mountain of work, but if you write just 1,000 words per day, you can write an entire book in 60 days! If you consider that a single page of typed text averages around 500 words, you only need to fill two pages per day. And if that still seems insurmountable, try writing 500 words (just one page) per day. You'll be done in four months.

To make the project seem even easier, take your outline and tackle it bit by bit. When you look at the project as a whole, it can seem overwhelming.

But if you commit to working on one subtopic per day, you will chisel away at it until you have a fabulous final product.

If you've previously written articles or special reports, you may already have a solid foundation for your first book by using those existing articles. Conversely, if you tackle your book by treating each section as an article or report, you will be surprised by how seamlessly your project can come together.

Another option is to solicit contributions from others. Whether you fill the entire book with contributions from others, or simply enhance the book by sprinkling it with articles by contributors, this can quickly increase the content and also add value to a book since people love real-world advice. Are you enjoying the profiles of the infopreneurs in this book? These stories enhance the overall value of the book while giving the contributors free exposure. It's a win-win for the author, the contributors, and readers.

IF YOU DON'T LIKE TO WRITE

Hiring a ghostwriter can be a solution for potential authors who either don't like or feel uncomfortable with the writing process. A contract should be drafted with the person you hire that outlines the form of payment and terms. Fees for ghostwriting are based on the writer's experience and the duration of the project. Some may charge an hourly fee or project-based fee. If the author has any kind of celebrity status, he may request credit for the work and even a percentage of the royalties.

Before you contact a writer, determine what the job is worth to you. Would you prefer to pay a flat fee up front or are you willing to carve out a piece of the royalties? Do you want the ghostwriter to be credited as an author of the book or do you wish for her name to remain silent? If you are unsure about how long your project will take, the writer should be able to assist you in coming up with a time line.

There are several options for locating potential ghostwriters:

- ✔ Post an ad on www.craigslist.org.
- ✔ Search www.allfreelancework.com, a directory of freelancers.
- ✔ Search www.elance.com, a directory of freelancers.

✔ Check out the writer profiles at www.freelancesuccess.com.

✔ Post a job listing at www.publishersmarketplace.com.

If you can speak your book, you can record the contents and hire someone to transcribe and edit it for you. Transcription services could end up being a fairly expensive option, but certainly a valid one if this method works for you. You might also want to consider investing in dictation software. These products work with your computer and can generate a written document based on your spoken words. Check out Dictation Buddy from www.highcriteria.com or Naturally Speaking from www.nuance.com.

FINDING A NICHE

Once you know what you want to write about, you need to locate any other books that exist on your topic. The easiest way is to search www.amazon.com for keywords on your topic. For example, if you want to write about how to start a consulting business, search the business books category for the following keywords:

✔ Consulting

✔ Coaching

✔ Advisor

✔ Start a [insert specialty such as financial planning, marketing, etc.] business

When you locate titles (and most likely you will), take note of the following:

✔ When was the book published?

✔ Is it still in print?

✔ What is the sales rank on Amazon? The lower the rank, the better the current sales of the title.

✔ What topics are covered in the table of contents?

✔ How good or bad are the reviews?

✔ Do the reviewers cite topics that were neglected?

✔ How well-known is the author?

✔ Are there topics that aren't covered that you think should be?

✔ How would your book be better?

Pick up a copy of each of the books in your area of expertise so you can better understand your competition. You don't necessarily want to emulate an existing book, but you need to understand what you're up against and identify a way to make yours different or better.

If the market is saturated with books on your topic, determine how you can narrow your focus. If you run a pet-sitting business, you could write a book called *How to Start a Profitable Pet Services Business* and include chapters on pet sitting, obedience training, grooming, and dog walking. If the market is oversaturated with books in this genre, you could change your focus to *How to Market a Pet Services Business* or *Real-World Advice from Pet Business Owners*.

Another option is to poll your potential audience. Ask business contacts and customers if they would be interested in reading a book like yours. Find out what kind of information they want to learn about. Study your market carefully before you proceed so you don't end up wasting your time on a book that has already been written or is well established.

Don't be discouraged if there already is a book out there that covers your topic. Most genres have multiple guides with similar topics (self-help books are a great example). With millions of readers in the world, there is certainly room for another guide as long as it takes a different approach.

GETTING STARTED

Just as you learned in school, you should start by outlining your book. The content should have a logical flow. One way to make this process easier is to use Post-it notes to map out your topics. Get a large board and write topic headings and subheadings on sticky notes. Place them in order and move them around until you are satisfied with the flow of information.

WRITING GOOD COPY

If you don't have writing experience, you may want to consider taking a class or two at the local college or adult learning center to develop your skills. Writing classes can help you develop your craft and can make the difference between a mediocre manuscript and a fabulous one.

There are also dozens of instructional writing books:

✔ *Bird by Bird: Some Instructions on Writing and Life* by Anne Lamott
✔ *On Writing Well* by William Zinsser
✔ *The Classic Guide to Better Writing: Step-by-Step Techniques and Exercises to Write Simply, Clearly and Correctly* by Rudolph Flesch

There are some basic rules when it comes to writing good copy. The following list is a primer:

✔ Grab your audience from the beginning by opening with attention-getting prose.
✔ Minimize your words. Write your first draft, then slice and dice it. It can be painful to cut words off the pages, especially after you've put your heart and soul into them, but tight writing means that you get your point across in as few words as possible.
✔ Beware of long paragraphs. Today our society is in a hurry and looking at long paragraphs is the equivalent of getting stuck in a conversation with a long-winded person. Paragraphs should be short to keep the reader engaged.
✔ Use headings and subheadings just as I'm doing with this book. This helps break up your content and makes it easier to read.
✔ Use bullets, charts, and diagrams whenever possible. Make the text visually appealing.
✔ Vary your sentences. Write short sentences and then write longer sentences. This is a powerful technique. Notice how the prior sentence grabs you because it is shorter, and this one is much longer so you have more to digest. A short sentence can make a point. Mixing up your sentences can make your writing more engaging.
✔ Use anecdotes and examples. If you are describing how to do something, an example can make it easier to understand. It can also make it more entertaining to read.
✔ Use dialogue whenever possible. Injecting quotes from people you have interviewed will make your pages more interesting. People also love to learn from those who have been there before.

✔ Insert facts and figures. If you're on top of your industry's trends, it should be easy for you to locate compelling statistics. Cite the sources of any statistics you include.

✔ When using terminology that not everyone has heard before, make sure to define the terms.

✔ When describing how to accomplish something, think of it as writing a recipe. You wouldn't tell the reader to put the cake in the oven before you've listed the ingredients for the batter. When describing how to do something, list the steps in the most logical order.

✔ If you aren't already a reader, it's time to become one. Reading can make you a better writer because not only will you learn from others, but you will automatically develop your skills as a wordsmith.

WHAT'S IN A NAME?

The title of your book is almost as important as the content. The title is often your first opportunity to grab a potential buyer's interest. For nonfiction books, it's best to stick with a descriptive title so readers instantly know what the book is about. A bit of play on words is okay, as long as the theme is still obvious. You can also use a subtitle to further describe the content. Here are some examples of catchy and descriptive titles:

✔ *Good to Great: Why Some Companies Make the Leap and Others Don't* by Jim Collins

✔ *The Art of the Start: The Time-Tested, Battle-Hardened Guide for Anyone Starting Anything* by Guy Kawasaki

✔ *Patent it Yourself* by David Pressman

✔ *How to Buy, Sell, and Profit on eBay: Kick-Start Your Home Based Business in Just 30 Days* by Adam Ginsburg

✔ *Starting an Online Business for Dummies* by Greg Holden

Make a list of at least 10 potential titles and subtitles. Move words around until you narrow it down to three or four options. Next, survey colleagues, friends, and family and ask for their opinions. Most important, check to see if the title is already in use by another author. Visit Amazon.com to search for titles and make sure yours is unique. It may take weeks or even months to settle on a title for your book, but it's worth the investment in your time. You may also find inspiration for your title while writing your book. Be patient with the process and the right title will come to you.

SOLICIT FEEDBACK

Good writers know that feedback is critical to the writing process. Even the wildly successful author Stephen King shares his initial manuscripts with a few close and discerning friends.

Enlist some trusted readers to give you feedback on your manuscript. The challenge here is getting objective opinions. Your spouse or best friend may prefer to tell you what you want to hear, so make it clear that you want honest opinions. Opinions are also subjective and you may not necessarily agree with the feedback you receive. If several readers make similar comments, however, you should probably take their responses seriously.

To get valuable feedback, encourage your reviewers to make notations on a hard copy of the manuscript. You may even want to provide a list of questions for your reader to answer for you. Take the opportunity to probe about any concerns you have with your content. Here are some sample questions:

- ✔ How well does the information flow?
- ✔ Are there any areas that need to be revised?
- ✔ Are there any concepts that are unclear or confusing?
- ✔ What sections do you like best?
- ✔ Are there any sections that should be omitted?
- ✔ Is there any information that should be added?
- ✔ Did the book leave you with any unanswered questions?
- ✔ What was your overall impression of the book?

You may also want to consider joining a writer's group. These groups bring writers together and help them develop their craft. Each group is different. Some groups simply talk about writing, while others critique each other's work. You can find tremendous support from groups like these. Check with your local bookstore, library, and calendar listings in the newspaper to locate groups in your area, or start a group of your own.

Writer's conferences and workshops can also offer tremendous value. Visit Shaw Guides (http://writing.shawguides.com) for an excellent directory of events.

Infopreneur Profile

Joe Vitale
Hypnotic Marketing Inc.
Wimberley, Texas
www.mrfire.com

PUBLICATIONS:

- *The Attractor Factor: 5 Easy Steps for Creating Wealth (or Anything Else) from the Inside Out* (hardcover, $24.95)
- *There's a Customer Born Every Minute: P. T. Barnum's Amazing 10 Rings of Power for Creating Fame, Fortune, and a Business Empire Today—Guaranteed* (hardcover, $24.95)
- *The Greatest Money-Making Secret in History* (paperback, $13.95)
- *Life's Missing Instruction Manual: The Guidebook You Should Have Been Given at Birth* (hardcover, $19.95)
- *The Seven Lost Secrets of Success* (paperback, $19.95)
- Several additional books, including some that are co-written with other authors

What other products and services do you sell?

- More than thirty eBooks including *Idea Gold: How to Generate Ideas That Turn into Money* ($19.95), *Hypnotic Writing: The Underground Classic That Started It All* ($37.00), and *How to End Self-Sabotage for Aspiring eBook Authors* ($29.95).
- Several audio and video programs including *The Attractor Factor Blueprint Essential DVD Study Course* ($497.00) and *Money Beyond Belief* ($49.00).
- Joe also sells a variety of other items including software, branded t-shirts and mugs, a membership newsletter, and a mentoring program.

Who is your target audience for your materials?
Self-employed solo entrepreneurs and Internet entrepreneurs.

How did you begin your infopreneur business?
My first eBook was *Hypnotic Writing* (www.hypnoticwriting.com). I didn't think anyone would buy an eBook. I was wrong. I sold 600 overnight at $30.00 each. I tasted ecstasy.

Where do you sell your products?
Primarily online.

How do you market your materials? What marketing strategies have and haven't worked?
Through offers to my mailing list, and my affiliates send their lists. I also use news releases to get media to send people and write articles that lead people back to my site.

You're published with a major publishing house. How did you secure your first book deal?
I got an introduction from a professional author who liked my work.

What has been the most challenging part of your business?
Doing everything myself.

What has been the most rewarding part of your business?
Making money while I sleep and changing lives with good information.

What have you learned from your business experience that you would like to share with others?
Act on ideas fast, money likes speed. Don't delay, doubt, or second guess. Get things done. Let the market decide.

Looking back, is there anything you would do differently?
I would have taken action sooner on my products and not wasted time wondering if they would work.

CHAPTER

4

Go Big: How to Get Published Traditionally

This is the sixth book I've written, which isn't bad for a guy who's only read two.

—GEORGE BURNS

Perhaps the best news about seeking a traditional publisher for a non-fiction book is that the book doesn't have to be completely written before you begin the search. In fact, most literary agents and publishers expect to see only two or three sample chapters along with a proposal and an outline of the book before making a decision to sign a contract with an author. Once a publishing contract is signed, the author and publisher agree to a date when a complete manuscript is due.

To break into the competitive publishing industry, you need a great idea, a lot of persistence, preparation, and a little luck. The road to traditional publication is a long process that requires the following 11 steps:

1. Develop your platform for book sales.
2. Decide on an idea for a book.
3. Define your target audience so you know you have a market for the book.

4. Evaluate the competition.

5. Write a comprehensive proposal and at least two sample chapters.

6. Contact agents until you find one willing to represent you (and one who is excited about your project).

7. Find a publisher (either with the help of an agent or on your own).

8. Negotiate a contract and sign a deal.

9. Finish writing your book by the due date outlined in your contract.

10. Proceed through the editing process, which can take months to complete.

11. Launch the new book and market the heck out of it.

LITERARY AGENTS

A literary agent acts as a liaison between an author and a publishing house. Literary agents take a percentage of the book deals that they make, which typically amounts to 10 percent of U.S. rights and 15 percent if they sell foreign rights (the rights for your book to be published in another country). Many agents also charge back to clients for photocopying and shipping. Reputable agents do not charge fees to read a book proposal or manuscript so beware of any agent who requires a fee up front.

Once an author signs a contract with an agent, the agent helps the author fine-tune the proposal and prepare it for submission to publishers. When the proposal is ready, the agent sends it to publishing contacts and navigates the negotiation process and contract terms.

The agent and the author have the same goal: to get the largest book advance possible. An advance is what the publisher pays the author in anticipation of book sales. The publisher estimates how much revenue the book sales will generate and bases the advance on that figure. Authors won't earn any royalties on book sales until the advance is earned back. Once that happens, royalties are paid to the author based on a percentage agreed to in the author's publishing contract, with rates ranging from 8 percent to 15 percent of either the wholesale or retail price of the book. For new authors, a book advance can be as low as $2,500. Some well-known authors receive advances well into six figures.

While most small and midsize publishers accept book proposals directly, the largest publishing houses only work with literary agents. If you want to receive a book advance and get published with a big house, then you will likely need an agent.

FINDING AN AGENT

Each agent has a special interest and focuses on books in certain genres. This preference usually reflects the agent's personal reading taste and her contacts at various publishing houses. You are asking for rejection if you send a proposal for a cookbook to an agent who specializes in children's books, so you need to research an agent before wasting your time as well as the agent's time with an inappropriate pitch.

Authors should keep in mind that agents need them as much as authors need the agents. The agents earn their living off their authors and therefore want to work with the ones who appear to have the most potential for sales. Part of this equation is dictated by the publishers. Publishers don't like to gamble on new authors unless there is a compelling reason to do so.

Most of the large publishing houses, and therefore agents, seek authors with a built-in platform. A platform is essentially the author's ability to sell the book. The publisher wants to know if the author is well known and has a stable audience of buyers. A good author platform means that the author has a national presence through speaking engagements, Internet exposure, or other celebrity status. Previous media exposure is also helpful. Has the author been on TV, radio, or in print? Without a platform, it is far more difficult to convince big publishers to take a chance on a new author. Small and midsize publishers, however, may still consider a new author if the book idea is convincing enough.

Many agents have web sites that detail their submission requirements so that authors know what to send. In most cases, agents want to see a query letter first so they can get an idea of what your book is about and whether it is a good fit for them.

Some agencies accept queries via e-mail, whereas others require them through postal mail with a self-addressed stamped envelope so they can return a response. A query letter should include a brief synopsis of the book with a solid hook. This is your chance to convince the agent that there is an audience for the book and that you are the person to write about the subject. Include a brief author bio detailing your qualifications for writing the book. You don't necessarily have to be an expert on a subject to write about it, but if you're not, you should have statistics and interviews from sources who are.

An agent who is intrigued by your query letter will request a book proposal and sample chapters, so be sure you have these items ready to go before you send out any query letters.

CONTACTING PUBLISHERS DIRECTLY

There are hundreds of small and midsize publishing houses that may be willing to consider your book without the assistance of an agent. The best way to locate these is to examine books in your genre. Find out who is publishing the majority of books in your subject area and begin researching your options. Most publishers have web sites where they detail what they expect from the submission process.

There are also two major publisher's organizations where you can locate a directory of publishers: Publishers Marketing Association (www .pma-online.org) and the Small Publishers Association of North America (www.spannet.org).

USING A QUERY LETTER

To contact publishers directly, you can use a query letter that is similar to the query letter you would write an agent. The following is adapted from a query letter that helped author Romanus Wolter sell his manuscript to John Wiley & Sons:

Sample Query Letter

Hi [name of person],

I would love to speak with you about my new book *Kick Start Your Success* and its ability to become a market phenomenon. I created this book to "compel people to take the right action for their success—now!"

I respect your time. Please feel free to call me at anytime to discuss the possibilities. My cell number is xxx and my work number is xxx.

Many people are overwhelmed with the challenges they face in their lives and in their careers. They are searching for action steps they can take to move forward on their dreams.

Kick Start Your Success is a short, wise book. I have listed below a few powerful best sellers that are similar in length to *Kick Start Your Success* (without a foreword or an index: approximately 90 pages). These books became classics simply by making a difference in people's lives.

As my friends, family, colleagues, and clients constantly remind me people want to know what action steps they can take today to achieve success:

- ***Kick Start Your Success* enables people to move forward on their ideas in just in one sitting.** We all have the capacity to carve out two to four hours in a weekend or late one night. Otherwise, it seems as if "life always gets in the way of my dreams."
- **Its action steps apply to life, career, and business.** *Kick Start Your Success* creates a solid foundation from which people can achieve life, career, and business goals. Since readers will most likely write in the book—they will buy another copy for their next goal.
- **Penetrating the "gift" market.** We want to help people, especially our loved ones, succeed but do not want to overwhelm them. People will buy *Kick Start Your Success* for themselves and additional copies for their friends and family enabling them to achieve their dream goals by inspiring others to help them.
- **Engaging today's audience.** We have become accustomed to receiving information quickly via television and the Internet. People will carry this compact book with them as they work on their goals, creating even greater word-of-mouth advertising.
- **Exciting the press.** Members of the press are used to getting succinct information—they must instantly attract audience interest. This is precisely why the 80-page *On Bullshit* by Harry Frankfurt is attracting a great deal of attention (number 3 on Amazon.com and over 200,000 copies sold) due to its length and its content.

I am passionate about making this short, powerful version a reality. My "work in the trenches" indicates that the book will be a best seller. "Up next on Oprah—Kick Start Your Success: Helping you create a solid foundation for your goal in just one hour!"

I would love to become part of the (Publisher's name) family because of your dedication to the authors you serve. Please feel free to call me at anytime to discuss the possibilities—my cell is xxx.

Possibilities,

Romanus
"The Kick Start Guy"

www.kickstartguy.com

RESOURCES FOR FINDING AGENTS AND PUBLISHERS

- ✔ *Writer's Market* by Kathryn S. Brogan
- ✔ *Jeff Herman's Guide to Book Publishers, Editors, and Literary Agents* by Jeff Herman
- ✔ The Association of Authors Representatives (a member-based organization for agents who follow a defined code of conduct) www.aar-online.org/mc/page.do
- ✔ Publisher's Marketplace (offers a directory of agents) http://www .publishersmarketplace.com
- ✔ Predators and Editors (an online directory of literary agents, including warnings about agents who aren't reputable) http://www .anotherealm.com/prededitors

Go to the bookstore or library to check out books in your genre. Most authors give a special thanks to their agent or editor in the acknowledgments section.

ELEMENTS OF A BOOK PROPOSAL

A good book proposal should be convincing, fully edited for spelling and grammatical errors, and thorough. Keep in mind that your proposal reflects you and your professionalism, so you want to make sure it is high quality and follows industry standards. Proposals can range from 10 to 50 pages.

A proposal should have the following elements:

- ✔ It should be typed on 8.5 × 11 white standard bond paper.
- ✔ Contents should be double-spaced.
- ✔ A footer should indicate the author's name and book title.
- ✔ Pages are numbered consecutively.
- ✔ Use a standard font, such as Times New Roman, in 12-point size for easy reading.
- ✔ The proposal should not be stapled or bound with anything other than a large binder clip.

The following is an outline you can use to create your book proposal:

- ✔ **Cover page:** This should include the book title, subtitle, author name, estimated word count for the final book (typically 60,000 to 80,000 words), and author's contact information (address, phone number, e-mail address, and web site URL).

- ✔ **Overview:** Two to five pages that highlight the most important elements of the book. Your first few paragraphs are your best chance to hook the agent or editor. If these aren't engaging, the rest of your proposal may not be read. Explain why the world needs this book, what the book is about, and why you are the best person to write it. If you can obtain any endorsements from celebrities or well-known authors, list them.

- ✔ **Market analysis:** One or two pages that explain who your target readers are. Are you targeting mothers, realtors, or business owners? Baseball fans, dog owners, or teenagers? List any recent statistics that support your case for a broad audience.

- ✔ **Competitive analysis:** List at least five books that would compete with your title. Explain the strengths and weaknesses of each and how your book will be different or better. Make sure to cite the author, publisher, and date of publication for each book. If you haven't read your competitors' books, you will need to before completing this section. It is also a great way to help you structure your book since evaluating the competition is sure to give you some ideas for how to make your book better.

✔ **Promotion plan:** Two or more pages that describe how you will market this book. This is an important element of your proposal so put a lot of thought and substance into this section. List any media experience and contacts that you have. Indicate if you write articles for magazines or if you regularly perform any type of public speaking.

Most publishers don't spend much money to promote new authors. You can offer to do a book tour, but will most likely have to fund the tour yourself. If you have a significant amount of money that you plan to contribute to promotion efforts, indicate this here by saying, "The author is willing to match the publisher's promotion budget up to $xx.xx." If you plan to spend less than $10,000, leave this statement out.

✔ **Chapter outline:** Include chapter titles and key points for each chapter. This can be a bulleted list or several paragraphs describing each chapter.

✔ **Author bio:** Give a brief overview of your qualifications, previous writing credits, and anything that will justify why you are a good person to write this book. This is not the place to list your hobbies, pets, or other irrelevant details. Stick to the topic at hand and demonstrate your authority on the subject. Most important, if you have a large following (huge mailing list, regular speaking engagements, etc.), make sure you indicate it here.

✔ **Delivery information:** This is a short paragraph that lists the estimated word count of the completed manuscript, the number of months needed to complete the manuscript, and how the manuscript can be delivered (via a Word document on disk is preferable).

✔ **Sample chapters:** Include one to three sample chapters.

✔ **Supporting documentation:** Include copies of published articles, publicity materials, and anything that demonstrates the author's talents, accomplishments, and promotional abilities.

PUBLISHING CONTRACTS

If a publisher offers you a contract, get ready for your head to spin. These contracts can vary greatly in what they offer and what they expect from the author. In general, a contract will outline the following:

PAYMENT TERMS

As mentioned, a book advance fee ranging from $2,500 to $10,000 is most typical for first-time authors. Authors with a successful track record can expect significantly higher advances. Advances are often paid over time; some publishers pay half at contract signing, and half after the manuscript is accepted (after the final editing process is complete). Some pay in thirds: one-third on contract signing, one-third on acceptance, and one-third when the book is published.

Royalty rates are paid after the book earns back the initial advance. Then royalties are paid based on a percentage of the book's retail, or more commonly, wholesale price. Typical percentages are 8 percent to 15 percent of the wholesale price; the percentage may increase on a tiered scale depending on the number of books sold.

The terms for sales of foreign rights, audio, or book club rights are typically split 50/50 between the publisher and the author. For example, if the publisher sells the rights to reprint your book in France for $2,000, it will deduct any related expenses and split the remaining balance with you.

RIGHTS

Generally, when you sign a contract with a publisher, you are giving up much of the control over your work. The contract may require that you do not reprint any portion of your manuscript in any other format. You may be allowed to use portions of the text for reprinting in magazines or other promotional venues. The publisher may also request the right to change the title of your book and often will have full control over your book's cover design.

The publisher will also specify the amount of time it has to publish your book. This time frame can range from 12 months to three years. If it doesn't publish within the agreed time frame, you have the right to cancel your contract.

You will also be involved in the editing process. Your manuscript will be reviewed by a copy editor and sent to you with requests for revisions. This process can take months, and you may go back and forth several times before you receive the final copy for approval.

If you are lucky enough to receive a book contract offer, use due diligence and hire an attorney, agent, or book shepherd who can help you review the terms of the contract. Whenever you sign your name to any legal document, you should be well informed and know exactly what you're getting into. Determine what criteria are most important to you, and don't be afraid to ask for some changes. The publisher may or may not be willing to negotiate, but you won't know unless you ask.

ADDITIONAL RESOURCES

- ✔ *How to Write a Book Proposal* by Michael Larsen.
- ✔ *Write the Perfect Book Proposal: 10 Proposals That Sold and Why* by Jeff Herman and Deborah Levine Herman.
- ✔ *Guerrilla Marketing for Writers: 100 Weapons to Help You Sell Your Work* by Jay Conrad Levinson, Michael Larsen, and Rick Frishman.
- ✔ Jenna Glatzer is a freelance writer and author of several books. She offers a sample book proposal on her web site: www.absolutewrite .com/novels/book_proposal1.htm.

Infopreneur Profile

Romanus Wolter
"The Kick Start Guy"
San Francisco, California
www.kickstartguy.com

PUBLICATIONS:

- *Kick Start Your Success* (John Wiley & Sons, $19.95)
- *Kick Start Your Dream Business* (Ten Speed Press, $18.95)

Editor's note: *Kick Start Your Dream Business* was originally self-published. Wolter later took his successful sales numbers and sold the publishing rights to Ten Speed Press.

BRIEF DESCRIPTION OF CONTENTS:

The books provide action steps that close the gap between goals and success. *Kick Start Your Success* is just the kick-in-the-pants people need to accomplish anything. It catapults you from "I want" to "I will" to "I did it."

Who is your target audience for your materials?
New moms, High School students, HR departments, dreamers and entrepreneurs, and the self-employed.

Where do you sell your materials?
On my own web site, online directories, stores, entrepreneurial sites, and Amazon.com. Also in major bookstores and at conferences.

When did your first publish your material?
1998.

What made you decide to self-publish?
I believe in the action steps I provide and follow them myself. The first step in selling a product (and yes, a book is a product) is to prove the market. I self-published to prove that my ideas worked and that people would buy them.

How does your publication enhance your business?
I call it a "huge business card." It shows what people will receive when they hire me as a consultant or invite me to a radio/television/Internet interview.

What was the process you used to publish?
Mmmm—is it too easy to say, "I just did it"? I produced the book, bartered with graphic designers to make it "pretty," and then bid it out to printers who had samples of books they did in the past. The funny thing is—when the book was picked up for national publication, they used many of my graphic elements because they were proven.

How do you market your materials?

Every marketing effort you do works on some level—never beat yourself up. The main goal is to inspire others to speak about you and your book. I speak at conferences, write for magazines (*Entrepreneur* magazine's Success Coach), and put articles on the Web.

What has been the most challenging part of the publishing process?

Again, my belief is that you just do it. I say, "Dream like a Child, Decide as an Adult." Set your goal and like a child, explore the possibilities—and ask for help. Then use your intuition and experience to take action as an adult. You will discover the right way to accomplish your goal.

What has been the most rewarding part of the publishing process?

When other people thank you for your words—how they have enhanced or changed their lives, their businesses, and their careers.

What have you learned from the experience that you would like to share with others?

Don't wait—go spread the word about your expertise. Believe in yourself, your words, and your ability to enhance people's lives; it will empower your actions.

Looking back, is there anything you would do differently?

Every action I have taken has brought me to where I am—and it is a wonderfully productive, enlightened, fun place.

CHAPTER

Do It Yourself: Self-Publishing Demystified

There is only one good way to defeat the enemy, and that is to write as well as one can. The best argument is an undeniably good book.

—SAUL BELLOW

There was a time when it was relatively easy to get a book published. You took a great idea to an agent, the agent sold the idea to a publisher, and soon you could call yourself an author. Now, the market has shifted. Unless you are a celebrity or come to the table with an eager audience of book buyers, most agents and big publishing houses won't even blink your way no matter how great your idea.

Because of this shift in the industry, more and more writers are turning to self-publishing. Some big success stories have emerged from the trenches of previously unknown authors who took control of their publishing destinies. *What Color Is Your Parachute?* by Richard Nelson Bolles, *The Celestine Prophecy* by James Redfield, and *The One Minute Manager* by Ken Blanchard and Spenser Johnson, all started out as independents. Even the infamous Amy Fisher turned to print on demand when she published her memoir, reportedly so that she could retain control over the content and promotion while earning a bigger percentage of the profits.

Profits can be another advantage of doing it yourself. When you publish with a traditional publisher, you will be lucky to receive 8 percent to 15 percent of the wholesale price in royalty payments. That can equate to just $0.80 to $2.00 per book sold. When you publish yourself, you can control many of the costs and ultimately earn $2.00 to $15.00 per book, depending on your price point and how well you manage the costs.

SELF-PUBLISHING OPTIONS

If you are considering publishing a book, you have two primary options: self-publishing and print on demand (POD). Basic self-publishing involves establishing your own publishing company, contracting a cover designer, laying out the interior of the book, and purchasing an International Standard Book Number (ISBN). Once the setup is complete, you can then have the book printed by a bookbinding company—usually in large quantities of 2,000+ at a cost per book ranging from $1.00 to $5.00. Once the book is published, you need to get it listed with the online book sellers and with the large distributors if you want your title to have a chance of making it into the big bookstores.

Print on demand companies charge a setup fee ranging from $350 to $1,500 and most will lay out the interior of the book, assign an ISBN number, print books on an as-needed basis (no major quantity purchases are required), and get them listed with the major distributors (Ingram and Baker & Taylor) and online booksellers.

Depending on your goals, POD or traditional self-publishing can allow you to convert your manuscript into a hardcover or trade paperback in a matter of weeks. It can take a year or more for a big-name publisher to transform a manuscript into a book, and author royalties can be surprisingly low. Publishing yourself gives you control over the time to market and can also lead to hefty profits. Here are some additional considerations.

SELF-PUBLISHING PROS

- ✔ You keep control over all rights.
- ✔ Individual book cost is low, resulting in a higher profit margin.
- ✔ Once you set up your publishing company, it's a bit easier to print subsequent books.

SELF-PUBLISHING CONS

- ✔ You have to do all the work: establish a publishing company, purchase an ISBN, get the cover created, lay out the text, get listed with distributors, and so on.
- ✔ Start-up costs can be high since you typically have to purchase a large quantity of books.
- ✔ Revisions can be expensive if you haven't yet sold the bulk of your initial inventory.

PRINT ON DEMAND PROS

- ✔ Start-up costs are lower since you only pay a setup fee and for as many copies as you need.
- ✔ Updating the book is more cost-effective since you won't have hundreds of overstock copies in your storeroom.
- ✔ Most POD companies will get your title listed with distributors and booksellers.

PRINT ON DEMAND CONS

- ✔ Profit margin is lower since the POD companies take a percentage of sales.
- ✔ Some contracts can be restrictive with rights and terms (contracts should be carefully reviewed).
- ✔ Reputation can be a challenge. The big bookstores don't yet regard POD books as having much credibility so authors must work twice as hard to prove their worth.

LESSONS LEARNED FROM THE PUBLISHING INDUSTRY

You may still want to investigate selling your idea to a big publisher, and you should. The process of pitching a book idea to agents and editors can teach you a lot about the publishing industry. The first question you will be asked is, "What is your platform?" Agents and publishers want authors with a ready-made audience of book buyers, and if you don't have a national presence with speaking engagements or other notoriety, it will reduce your chances of being published the traditional way.

But don't let the pitching process kill your dreams. The lesson you can take away from the publishing pros is that you need to have a way to market and sell your book. Before you even consider publishing yourself, develop a marketing plan. Determine who will buy your book and how you will reach your audience. If you know how to market your ideas and use the resources at your disposal (how-to books and publishing web sites), you can create your own self-publishing success story.

STEPS TO SELF-PUBLISHING

To start a self-publishing business, you need to complete the following 13 basic steps:

1. **Form a publishing company.** Starting a publishing company essentially equates to launching a new business. You need to first decide on a business name and then make sure the name is not already taken. Depending on the size of your company now and in the future, you should verify that the business name you choose is not already trademarked. Each state has different regulations for corporation names, so if you intend to incorporate, you will need to check with the secretary of state's office to search for existing corporations with your selected business name. Even if you don't plan to incorporate right away, you could change your mind in a few years, and it will be frustrating and costly to change your business name.

If you are a sole proprietor or a partnership, you will have to register a fictitious business name, which banks require to set up a business bank account. Fictitious business names also have to be published in a newspaper, notifying the public and allowing other business owners the opportunity to contest the name you have filed. While you can use a business name that is already in use in another state, you cannot use it if the business name has a trademark. Infringing on a trademark is illegal and will make you vulnerable to lawsuits from the trademark owner. Perform a free trademark search by visiting the United States Patent and Trademark Office (www.uspto.gov).

2. **Establish a form of ownership.** Whether to incorporate your publishing business is an important decision that depends on several factors:

how much personal liability you have in the business, how much income you generate, and how your tax payments are structured. You should consult with an accountant or attorney to determine the most appropriate choice. The following is a brief overview of the different business structures:

✔ **Sole proprietor:** A sole proprietor is responsible for all liabilities and debts in a business, and also receives the profits and assets generated by the business. The law views a sole proprietor and the business essentially as one and the same. It is the simplest type of business structure and all profits are reported as personal income, which can be a disadvantage if the business makes a substantial amount of money.

✔ **Partnership:** A partnership can be established when two or more people share ownership of a business. In this case, the partners need to have a legal agreement drafted that defines the division of profits and assets, how much each partner will contribute in capital, how disputes will be resolved, provisions for adding partners and how the business should be dissolved or bought out by a partner.

A legal agreement is important because, like any relationship, not all business partners are good matches and the situation could eventually change. Like sole proprietors, partners and the business itself are viewed as one entity by the law. There are three types of partnerships:

1. **General partnership:** A joint venture that is typically shared equally (unless otherwise stated in the legal agreement), with equal division of profits, losses, and responsibilities.

2. **Limited partnership:** This form of partnership generally specifies that the participants have limited liability and also limits the input to management decisions. This structure may not work well for service or retail businesses and is best used for bringing in investors for short-term projects.

3. **Joint venture:** This structure is used for a short-term investment or project. If the partners continue working together on an ongoing basis, the structure must be changed to one of the other options.

✔ **Corporation:** A corporation is its own entity that is taxed, can be sued, and can enter into contractual agreements. The owners of a corporation are shareholders who elect a board of directors to oversee the major decisions and policies of the company. Since the corporation is its own entity, it can continue even when ownership changes hands.

Shareholders in corporations have less liability than sole proprietors; however, officers of the company can be held liable for legal matters such as failing to pay taxes or payroll. Corporations can deduct the cost of benefits for employees and officers, and can raise capital by selling shares of the company stock.

Incorporating requires significant paperwork, and corporations must comply with federal, state, and some local agencies. Dividends that are paid to shareholders are not deductible as business income, which can result in paying higher taxes.

✔ **Subchapter S corporation:** This is a tax election that allows a shareholder to treat profits as distributions that pass through to his or her personal tax return. The shareholder must be paid a salary that meets the standards of "reasonable compensation," meaning that the wages are comparable to what would be paid to someone in a similar position. If this is not done, the Internal Revenue Service (IRS) can reclassify the business and require the shareholder to pay taxes on all the profits and earnings.

✔ **Limited liability company (LLC):** A limited liability company is a relatively new structure that bridges the gap between a general partnership and a corporation, bringing together the protection from personal liability offered by corporations and the flexibility of a partnership.

The duration of an LLC is determined when the business is filed, though it can be extended if members agree. Limited Liability Companies must not have more than two of the four characteristics that define corporations: limited liability to the extent of assets; continuity of life; centralization of management; and free transferability of ownership interests.

Federal tax forms for LLCs are typically the same as the forms used for partnerships. However, if more than two of the characteristics that define a corporation exist, the business must file corporation forms.

Given the complexities, legal and tax ramifications, and benefits of each business structure, it is easy to see why it is important to consult with your accountant and attorney when making this important business decision. Visit www.irs.gov for additional resources.

3. Apply for licenses and permits. The business license requirements are different for each state and county. In general, you will likely need a basic business license that is renewed each year and will cost from $50 to $500 depending on where you live. You will also need a resale license, which allows you to purchase products at wholesale (without paying sales tax) and requires that you collect and report sales tax. When you apply for this license, your local government will provide you with the details on how to report and remit payment for the taxes you collect.

4. Hire an editor. Your book represents you, and not hiring an editor is probably the biggest mistake that self-published authors make. I have reviewed hundreds of independent books over the years and the ones that quickly lose credibility are those with grammar, spelling, and punctuation errors. These embarrassing mistakes not only can hurt your readership, but can prevent bookstores and reviewers from taking your work seriously.

No matter how meticulous you are or how many times your spouse proofreads your work, you can't catch all the errors. Make the wise investment of hiring a professional to make your manuscript as clean as possible.

5. Purchase an ISBN. An International Standard Book Number (ISBN) is a unique 10- or 13-digit number that is assigned to a book title for 30 years. Bowker (www.bowker.com) is the major governing agency that issues ISBN numbers, which must be purchased in blocks of 10, 100, 1,000, or 10,000 for $225, $800, $1,200, or $3,000, respectively. Each application takes 10 days to process before the numbers are issued. If necessary, you can pay an additional fee to have your application expedited.

6. Obtain a bar code. A special bar code called the Bookland EAN is needed along with your ISBN if you intend to sell your books through bookstores. The code electronically identifies your book's title and price information. Even if you aren't sure where you will sell your book, a bar code is an essential part of your cover and gives your book a professional appearance.

There are numerous services that can generate a bar code for you for a cost ranging from $10 to $30. Here are some resources:

✔ Bar Code Graphics: www.createbarcodes.com.

✔ A list of providers is available here: www.isbn.org/standards/home /lsbn/us/barcode.asp.

✔ If you intend to sell your books through nontraditional bookstore outlets such as grocery stores, you will need a Universal Product Code (UPC). The providers listed previously can also help in obtaining a UPC if needed.

7. Copyright your work. Simply putting a copyright statement on your written work means that others do not have the right to distribute or reproduce it. For just $30, however, you can register your copyright officially, which can help protect you legally if someone tries to "borrow" your work later on. Visit www.copyright.gov for details.

Make sure you also have copyright information after the title page in your book. The most important line is Copyright [date] and your name.

⚡ HOT TIP ⚡

To print the copyright symbol—the letter C with a circle around it—in Microsoft Word, type the letter C between two parentheses: (C). Word will automatically format the type into the copyright symbol: ©.

---

8. Register with the Library of Congress. The Library of Congress is a registry of books in print. Its catalog is used by libraries and subscribers to access books so if you want to make your book available to libraries, you need to apply for a Library of Congress Control Number (LCCN). When you register, you will be assigned a catalog number that should be printed in the copyright section of your book. Your book must be at least 50 pages long to be listed in the catalog. To apply online, visit http://pcn.loc.gov.

9. Determine book specifications and cover design. Perhaps the most common book size today is the trade paperback at 5.5″ × 8.5″. This is also the most economical choice for most books. You can opt to publish a hardcover volume, though you should expect a significant increase in cost. Given the industry shift toward trade paperback, this is often a good option. You may also want to publish a workbook or other oversized book. It is a good idea to talk with your printing company about your options early on.

The fact is that you *can* judge a book by its cover, so this is no time to skimp. Your cover is your best chance to make a first impression so you want a product that you can be proud of and that grabs the attention of readers.

It would be wise to hire a professional book cover designer—someone who has done this kind of work before. While a talented graphic artist could probably turn out something that is acceptable, a person who specializes in book covers will have a much better handle on the market.

Keep in mind that you want your title to be prominent and you will also want to include a description on the back cover (also known as jacket copy). Some authors include their photo and a brief bio. If you have any testimonials, this is a good spot for them.

To locate a book cover designer, check out freelance sites such as www.elance.com or www.allfreelancework.com. If you are a member of any publishing trade associations, you may also be able to locate a designer through their network. Be sure to ask to see a portfolio of work. You can expect to pay between $250 and $1,000 for a professionally designed book cover.

10. Select a book printer. There are literally dozens of book printers. You will want to select yours based on price, minimum quantity, and location, which are often related to each other. If you live in California, it may be difficult to get a competitive rate from a printer on the East Coast once you factor in the cost of shipping (books are heavy and therefore the cost of shipping can blow your budget). Each printer also has different specifications for print runs. Some may agree to print 1,000 books, and others will require a minimum order of 3,000 books. Be sure you are confident that you can sell whatever number of books you decide to print.

To obtain pricing, you will have to contact printers and request a quote. It is wise to contact several printers so you can compare your options. The printer will need to know your estimated number of pages, the size of the book, whether you want a hardcover or trade paperback, whether your interior is all black ink or requires color (this will be significantly more expensive), whether your cover is in color (it should be), and the quantity of books you plan to print.

Questions you should ask the printer:

✔ What is the minimum number of books I can order?

✔ How much will shipping cost?

✔ Are there any setup fees?

✔ Is payment required up front or do you provide credit terms? If so, what are they: net 30 or net 60?

✔ What kind of paper is used? (You will want to use a 50 or 60 lb stock for paperbacks.)

✔ What is the turnaround time?

✔ Are there any hidden fees?

✔ Can you provide me with references?

For a comprehensive list of book printers, visit www.bookmarket.com /101print.html.

11. Set a price for your book. Deciding on a price for your book is a delicate dance between consumer demand and profit. This decision will depend partly on your cost to produce your books. Once you have obtained your printer price quotes and have a good idea of the price per book, you can then determine your price.

Take a look at books in your genre to evaluate the current market price. Nonfiction often sells for more than fiction, so it is not unreasonable to price a 350-page trade paperback at $20.00 or even higher. But be careful not to limit your market by overpricing your book.

Also, you will have to offer hefty discounts to distributors and merchants. Most expect to purchase books at a wholesale rates of 40 percent to as much as 66 percent off the cover price. So when deciding on your price, be sure to leave enough room to offer a deep discount and still make a profit.

12. Lay out the interior. You can hire the services of a contractor to lay out your book's interior, or you can do it yourself using your word processing software (Microsoft Word) or another program such as Microsoft Publisher, QuarkXpress, or PageMaker. Your format needs to match the size of the book you are publishing.

Once you're ready to begin, take a look at some of the books on your shelf and notice how the layout is organized. There are a few standards to be aware of:

✔ Every book has a title page that includes the author's name.

✔ Include a table of contents (fill in the page numbers once the layout is complete).

✔ Include a copyright statement.

✔ Chapters usually begin on a right-hand page.

✔ The left-hand page facing a new chapter usually is not blank. If your text doesn't fit into the last page before a new chapter begins, use filler such as a tip, quote, picture or diagram.

✔ Standard fonts such as Times New Roman and Arial are most common. Using other fonts may make the book look unprofessional.

✔ Font size is important. You want the book to be easy to read, but since you're printing it yourself, you also want to be aware of page count. Smaller fonts mean fewer pages, so if you're trying to minimize the number of pages, reduce your fonts. If you want to increase the number of pages, use a larger font.

✔ Headings are shown in bold and may not necessarily be in the same font as the rest of the text.

✔ A page number and title of the book should be listed either in the heading or the footer of each page.

13. Utilize distributors and wholesalers. Most bookstores order from book distributors and wholesalers instead of placing orders directly with thousands of publishers each year. This system streamlines the book ordering and delivery process and makes it a crucial part of your plan for publishing success. Unless your book is listed with a distributor and wholesaler, your sales will truly be an uphill climb.

Most bookstores prefer to order from wholesalers due to the wide variety and discount structure. The two most influential wholesalers are Ingram and Baker and Taylor. Ingram sells the majority of books to bookstores and other retail outlets, while Baker and Taylor is the primary supplier of books to libraries.

It is difficult for individuals and small publishers to get listed with the major wholesalers directly. Instead you must use the services of a book distributor. Distributors will handle the storing, selling, and shipping of your books to the wholesalers, who in turn make your books available to stores. Distributors are more likely to work to sell your book, whereas wholesalers typically wait to receive an order.

Both the distributor and the wholesaler expect to take a percentage of the book sales. You can expect to give away between 55 and 66 percent of your retail price. It is a high price to pay—literally—but it is the way of the publishing game and the reason your retail price needs to allow you room to make a profit. Payment from both types of organization also varies, and many will only pay you quarterly.

Different distributors have varying specialties. Some may specialize in nonfiction or children's books, whereas others may specialize in cookbooks or business. Distributors can also be picky about the titles they represent, so you will most likely have to go through an application and evaluation process.

The bottom line is that if you want your book to sell through bookstores and libraries, you will need to establish a relationship with a distributor (preferably one who can make your title available to the major wholesalers— especially Ingram and Baker and Taylor).

For a list of distributors, visit www.bookmarket.com/distributors.html or www.bookzonepro.com/resources/morelinks/distwhole.html.

GETTING BACK TO SELF-PUBLISHING VERSUS PRINT ON DEMAND

As you can see, self-publishing involves many steps. If you have the time, initiative, and desire to take on the challenge, it can be a rewarding (and lucrative) experience. If the steps are too many for you, then print on demand may be a better option. Though your cost per book may be slightly higher, the time saved could be worth it.

If you decide to pursue POD publishing, evaluate your options carefully. Some POD companies may require you to sign a contract giving them exclusive rights to your book—something you probably don't want to give away. The most reputable POD publishers allow you to retain your own rights, so that if you later want to sell your book to a traditional publishing house or take your business elsewhere, you can do so easily.

Also beware of vanity publishers. These shady operators try to act like traditional publishers, convincing authors that their works have been *selected* for publication and then forcing authors to pay for the production costs. Some even offer a symbolic payment of $1 to show you that they are committed to publishing your book. Any business that offers you just $1 for your hard-earned work is not worth the bubble gum that you can buy with that bill. Avoid making the mistake of working with a vanity publisher by doing plenty of research before committing to any publishing agreement.

How you decide to publish your work is a personal decision that depends on your individual publishing goals. And no matter what publishing solution you choose, don't forget to market the heck out of your book. Books won't sell themselves—you have to help them sell!

ADDITIONAL RESOURCES

✔ For more information on self-publishing, visit Dan Poynter's web site: www.parapublishing.com. Poynter is the author of *The Self-Publishing Manual,* and his newsletter is loaded with resources and advice.

✔ For a good comparison of the leading POD companies, check out: www.publishondemand.net.

✔ Find a host of publishing resources at www.businessinfoguide .com/publishing.htm.

Infopreneur Profile

Dan Poynter
Para Publishing
Santa Barbara, California
www.parapublishing.com

PUBLICATIONS:

- *The Self-Publishing Manual* (15th edition, $19.95; resources, completely revised, all about writing, editing, printing, promoting, marketing, and distributing books; over 180,000 in print; a new book—with a track record)
- *Writing Nonfiction: Turning Thoughts into Books* ($14.95; how to pick your topic; break it down; do research; use writing tricks and

tips; evaluate your publishing options; and get into print faster, easier, and cheaper)

- *Successful Nonfiction* ($14.95)
- *Is There a Book inside You?* ($14.95)
- *The Older Cat* ($14.95)
- *Parachuting, The Skydiver's Handbook* ($19.95)
- *The Parachute Manual, Volume 1* ($49.95)
- *The Parachute Manual, Volume 2* ($49.95)
- *Expert Witness Handbook* ($39.95)
- And many more

TYPE OF PUBLICATIONS:

Some in hardcover, soft, audio, large print, and eBooks. All are self-published.

Who is your target audience for your materials?
Writers, publishers, sky divers, cat lovers, and others.

Where do you sell your materials?
Web site, distributor to book trade, catalog, stores, and so on.

When did your first publish your material?
1969.

How did your journey to become an infopreneur begin?
My first book was a 500-page, 2,000-illustration, technical book on parachutes. Realizing that no publisher would understand it or know where to sell it, I borrowed money and published myself.

If you're published traditionally, how did you secure your book deal(s)?
I have sold to publishers. They came to me.

How does publication enhance your business?
My books, reports, and so on help people do what they want to do faster, easier, and cheaper. My publications are my business.

What was the process you used to publish? Did you read books, hire someone for help, hire an editor, start a publishing company, purchase special software, and so on?

When I began in 1969, there were no books, PMA [Publishers Marketing Association] did not exist, and the only other authors were fiction writers and poets who did not understand nonfiction. I figured out the business on my own.

What other products and services do you sell?

Mailing lists, eBooks, special reports, seminars, and more!

How do you market your materials? What marketing strategies have and haven't worked?

We are web site centric. All information emanates from the site and my weekly e-zine, which has a circulation of 25,000. I also conduct dozens of speaking engagements each year.

What has been the most challenging part of the publishing process?

Managing the day-to-day excitement and trying to help all the people who contact me.

What has been the most rewarding part of the publishing process?

Being able to make a living at something that fascinates me.

What have you learned from the experience that you would like to share with others?

The information business is rewarding and growing. You can be part of it.

Looking back, is there anything you would do differently?

Hire staff sooner.

CHAPTER 6

eBooks and Special Reports: Make Money While You Sleep

A large income is the best recipe for happiness I ever heard of.
—JANE AUSTEN

Perhaps the greatest advantage of publishing eBooks and special reports is that the process can be relatively simple. Once your content is written and edited (the hardest part), you can have an electronic version available for sale in a matter of minutes. Customers like them because they offer instant gratification—no waiting for the UPS truck to arrive. And authors like them because once the electronic document is ready for sale, it can continue to generate revenue for years to follow with very little overhead.

The primary difference between an eBook and special report is length. Special reports can be as short as a single page. eBooks can be as short as 10 pages (and alternately still be called a special report) or as long as 400 pages. In fact, the terms *eBook* and *special report* can be used interchangeably.

Publicity Hound, Joan Stewart, has authored over 50 special reports with a variety of page lengths. She proudly admits that she chose not to publish a print book and instead produces special reports because she makes more money with them. Her reports currently sell for $10 each. Combined, they would be about the length of a book that she could probably sell for $20.00 to $25.00. It seems to me that she's made a wise decision.

eBook versions can be offered in addition to a print book. If you own the rights to your print book, you can sell it in electronic format and give your customers a choice. Some may prefer a book in print while others seek the instant gratification of immediate download. eBooks have the added advantage of being searchable by key word, making it easy for readers to locate specific information.

FORMATTING AND DELIVERY

The main tool you need to publish an eBook or special report is a word processing application. While there are a variety of eBook formats on the market, PDF (portable document format) documents are currently the most popular in the business community.

PDF compilers compress the format of documents and make them available to PC users, Mac users, and some handheld devices. Adobe Acrobat (www.adobe.com) is the most popular PDF compiler on the market. The software costs around $200, although you can use a free trial that allows you to create up to five documents.

There are free PDF creators available on the Internet, but that old adage of "you get what you pay for" can mean you could have problems with formatting. Adobe's version also offers special features such as document security. If necessary, you can set preferences in your document that prevent others from modifying the information, copying the text, or even printing it.

If you don't want to use a PDF creator, another option is to distribute your electronic products through a publishing company such as Book Locker (www.BookLocker.com), Lulu (www.lulu.com), or other electronic publishing services. The benefit of these companies is that they handle the entire ordering process, collect the buyer's payment, and deliver the download. The downside is that you will likely give up more of your profit and in some cases, your rights. Some eBook service providers request exclusive rights, meaning that you cannot sell or distribute your book through other channels.

Many web site shopping cart providers offer their own tools for electronic document delivery. One such company, www.1shoppingcart.com, offers an eBook distribution tool with its premium shopping cart package. Their technology allows you to set up a shopping cart and credit card processing on your web site and automate document delivery, making the purchase process seamless for your customers.

Another company that specializes in electronic document delivery and payment collection is Payloadz (www.payloadz.com). Payloadz offers different service level packages based on the volume of downloads you sell, and keeps a nominal percentage of each transaction. Payments are collected through PayPal while Payloadz handles delivery of your PDF or other type of file. This is an inexpensive and simple solution that I use for my own electronic document sales. Payloadz also offers affiliate sales programs and the ability to list your electronic documents for sale in their eBay store.

While you could use an inexpensive payment collection service such as PayPal, the challenge will be that PayPal doesn't have a method for automatically distributing electronic books. You would therefore have to manually distribute products by responding to payment notification e-mails, which means that your customers will be disappointed by the delay (remember, it's all about instant gratification) and you will be married to your computer while you try to keep up with your orders. Ideally, you should be able to sell and distribute your electronic products while you sleep or while on vacation.

In addition to offering your eBooks and special reports as electronic downloads, you may also want to offer them on CD. The challenge here is that you then need a way to reproduce the CDs, as well as a way to fulfill and ship orders. Many authors that I interviewed don't bother selling their eBooks on CDs simply because it requires extra work. They also note that most people buy eBooks for the instant gratification of immediate download.

eBOOK FORMATS AND COMPILERS

There are several eBook reader devices on the market and each uses different eBook formats. Table 6.1 lists the common formats currently being offered (the ones in bold type are currently the most popular formats).

Format	File Type	Platforms
Adobe Reader	.pdf	Windows PC, Macintosh, PalmOS PDA www.adobe.com/products/acrobat/readstep2.html
Microsoft Reader	.lit	Windows PC, Pocket PC—download the free RMR add-in for Word Perfect to create MS Reader eBooks www.microsoft.com/reader/developers/downloads/rmr.asp
Mobipocket	.prc	Windows PC, most PDAs—users can import PDF or Word documents. www.mobipocket.com
Palm Reader	.pdb	Windows PC, Macintosh, Pocket PC http://ebooks.palm.com/product/detail/19286
Hiebook	.kml	Hiebook device, Windows PC www.hiebook.com
HTML	.htm	Windows PC, Macintosh, Unix, Linux, anything with a browser (most PDAs require an additional reader, such as Mobipocket)

TABLE 6.1   Popular eBook Formats

For many businesses today, PDF format is sufficient for eBooks and special reports. But if you want to offer different formats, there are dozens of eBook compiler programs for consideration. Because each program has its own unique features and benefits, you must do some research to find the product that meets your individual needs. Here are some to get you started:

- ✔ eBook Edit Pro: www.ebookedit.com
- ✔ Desktop Author: www.desktopauthor.com
- ✔ Activ eBook Compiler: www.ebookcompiler.com
- ✔ eBook Generator: www.ebookgenerator.com

eBOOK LAYOUT

Your eBook should be easy to read and navigate with a logical flow of information. Make sure you have a cover page that includes the title, author, and a web site link. It's a good idea to also have a title page that repeats the title and author information and includes a copyright statement. My eBook would have the following copyright and contact information:

Simply putting a copyright statement on your written work means that others do not have the right to distribute or reproduce it. For just $30, however, you can register your copyright officially. Visit www.copyright.gov for details.

In addition to the cover page, title page, and copyright statement, your eBook may include the following:

✔ Table of Contents
✔ Chapters
✔ Directory of Resources (if applicable)
✔ Glossary of Terms (if applicable)
✔ Index (if necessary)
✔ Author Bio
✔ List of Additional Products
✔ Order Form

Make sure you align the headings of your content and carefully proof the entire document for consistency and errors. If you don't trust your own editing skills, hire someone to edit your content. There is nothing worse than paying for a product that is loaded with errors. If you want people to take your business seriously, you need to take it seriously.

⚡ HOT TIP ⚡

You can design your own logos and images to give your eBooks and special reports a professional look. Check out the eCover

Creator from Laughing Bird Software (www.logocreator.com) or eCover Generator (www.ecovergenerator.com). These programs allow you to create a snazzy two-dimensional image of a book or software box in just minutes.

SELLING eBOOKS ON AMAZON.COM

It can be relatively easy to list an eBook for sale on your own web site, but if you want to take your publishing venture to the next level and make it available on Amazon.com, you need to follow some specific steps.

Amazon requires eBook publishers to use the services of their partner, Lightning Source Inc. (LSI): www.lightningsource.com. Prior to registering as a customer with LSI, you have to acquire your own International Standard Book Number (ISBN). You'll need an ISBN for selling through this channel. The procedure for obtaining an ISBN was covered in Chapter 5.

Your eBook materials must be fully edited and ready to go since once you submit, you will be charged for any changes. LSI accepts eBooks in three formats: Adobe Acrobat (PDF), Microsoft Reader (LIT), and Palm Reader (PDB). The only limitation to the length or size of an eBook is that it must be less than 10 megabytes.

Once your book is formatted and you have obtained your ISBN, you can register with LSI. The application process requires you to enter your tax ID or Social Security number and a valid credit card. The good news is that the fee for book submission is just $25 and no other fees are charged unless you need to make changes to your file. Once registered, you will receive instructions for submitting your eBook file along with a contract agreement.

You will receive a proof of your file and after you've approved the final version, LSI will list your title in its catalog and make it available to large resellers including Amazon.com, Powell's Books, eBookMall, Diesel eBooks, and others.

As the publisher, you set the cover price of your eBook as well as the wholesale discount price. The wholesale discount must be at least 25 percent although most eBook publishers set their discounts at 50 to 55 percent. Fortunately, LSI doesn't take any additional percentage points since it is compensated by the book dealers. So if you set your retail price at $20.00 with a 55 percent discount, you will be paid $9.00 every time your book is purchased. Payments are distributed by LSI on a quarterly basis.

Once your title is listed with Amazon.com, you can update the description, add a graphic image, or post reviews on the book's listing page. To make changes, display your eBook listing on Amazon.com and look just below where the graphic image is displayed (or should be displayed if you don't have one). You should find a link that says "Publishers: Learn how customers can search inside this book." Click on the link, type in your Amazon login information, and you will be taken to a list of choices for updating the contents of your book's page. Amazon will typically update the changes you submit within a week.

Because LSI's contract is nonexclusive, the author retains all rights. This means that you can also make your eBook available directly from a shopping cart on your web site or distribute it through other channels. If you want LSI to allow you to sell the eBook from your site, you will have to sign up with its retailer program, which can be costly. Instead, you might want to consider using a document distribution package such as the one provided by Payloadz.com or a shopping cart system with autoresponders like the one offered by 1ShoppingCart.com.

As with any book that is published, the success of an eBook depends on the author's marketing efforts. Although the process of acquiring an ISBN number, formatting your eBook, and submitting it through LSI may seem tedious, the advantages can be great if you put some effort into marketing your materials. Imagine the credibility you can add to your publicity when you are interviewed by a newspaper or radio station and you can say, "My eBook is available on Amazon!"

ADDITIONAL RESOURCES

- ✔ Join the eBook community on Yahoo: http://groups.yahoo .com/group/ebook-community
- ✔ eBookMall offers manuscript conversion, the ability to list your book for sale, and other services: www.ebookmall-publishing.com
- ✔ eBooks N' Bytes lists resources for eBook compilers, publishers, distribution, and more: www.ebooksnbytes.com

Infopreneur Profile

C. Hope Clark
Phoenix, Arizona
www.fundsforwriters.com

PUBLICATIONS:

- *Grants for the Serious Writer* (4th edition, eBook, $8.95; provides guidance on the grant world and talks about how grants are written, judged, and awarded. Offers almost 500 grants devoted specifically for writers.)
- *The No Fee Contest Book* (3rd edition, eBook, $7.95; provides guidance on writing contests then provides 250 contests that do not charge an entry fee. Entry fees bother a lot of writers.)
- *Publishers for Poets* (eBook, $7.95, talks about options for poets in seeking markets and funds then offers 309 poetry markets.)
- *Funds for the Fiction Writer* (eBook, $7.95, 317 listings from contests to literary journals; from publishers to magazines, and guidance on where to find avenues for fiction.)
- *Markets for the Young Writer* (eBook, $7.95)
- *Short & Sweet: Markets for Fillers* (eBook, $7.95)
- *Funds for the Essayist* (eBook, $7.95)
- *Tis the Season* (eBook, $4.95)
- *The Shy Writer: The Introvert's Guide to Writing Success* (eBook, $6.95; trade paperback, $14.95)

Who is your target audience for your materials?
Novice to journeyman level writers and journalists seeking writing income, and people who are Internet savvy.

Where do you sell your materials?
My web site, affiliate programs on other web sites, Amazon, and Barnes & Noble.

What made you decide to self-publish?
My books are work-related and link-intensive and waiting for the traditional route would mean my material would be dated.

How does your publication enhance your business?

The books draw people to my newsletters where I notify them of new eBook releases—a cycle of sorts.

What was the process you used to publish?

I read up on designing eBooks and I create them from scratch. I have a proofreader on hire as well as a cover designer whom I've worked a quantity deal with to make the original art work very affordable. My one trade paperback, *The Shy Writer*, is published by a company that specializes in print on demand, booklocker.com.

How do you market your materials?

I created an affiliate program—www.fundsforwriters.com/affiliates.htm—which works well. I also advertise through my newsletters that reach 14,000 writers. I swap ads with other newsletters, which also works very well.

What has been the most challenging part of the publishing process?

Keeping the material updated. I update the books at least annually if not semi-annually. With the number of books I carry, that makes for substantial work. Also, I am always coming up with a new title, which keeps people coming back. This tempts them to purchase another book they've thought about but haven't bought. Many more writers now buy more than one book—the latest one and one of the older ones.

What has been the most rewarding part of the publishing process?

Instant gratification and income stream. Plus, I'm in total control of the eBook sales.

What have you learned from the experience that you would like to share with others?

There isn't a business out there that cannot capitalize on eBooks. It's been a pretty good income for me from my personal study at home.

Looking back, is there anything you would do differently?

I would not have published my first paperback back in 2000. It had links in it and it became obsolete very fast.

Other Information Products: More Money in the Bank

Fortune favors the brave.

—VIRGIL, *AENEID*

Books, eBooks, and special reports are arguably the most common information products on the market, yet there are plenty of additional ways to generate income from information. This chapter examines some of these opportunities.

Since everybody has different interests and talents, not all of these strategies may be right for you. Be sure to spend some time deciding which options fit your overall goals best. You don't need to offer every type of product to be successful. You need only to offer the highest quality products that you can deliver, and for you, that may include just one or two types of information products.

TELESEMINARS

An informational seminar conducted on the telephone is known as a teleseminar. The host reserves a conference call line with a teleconference service provider and attendees dial in to the designated phone number to listen to the call. Some teleseminars are interactive and allow the audience to participate by asking questions. Others require that the audience is muted while the host does most of the talking or interviews a guest expert.

Many savvy Internet marketers host teleseminars. Some give free dial-in access to lure listeners into buying their products. Others offer meaty content and charge admission to the call—typically $10 to $35.

As with any information product, hosting successful fee-based teleseminars requires that you have access to a broad audience of potential customers and have a topic that people want to hear about badly enough to part with their money.

For content ideas, consider giving how-to presentations or interviewing an expert on a popular topic. Many experts are happy to participate in calls like these for free, although just as many will ask to split the revenues with you. This is where partnership agreements come in handy. The presentation can be beneficial to both parties if each of you has the opportunity to make money from the product sales, so be flexible when approaching others about participating. Your interviewee may also be willing to promote the call to his mailing list and help improve attendance, so the alliance can be worth the effort.

You can choose to allow the audience to ask questions during the call or to e-mail questions to you in advance. Manage the process of live questions by letting listeners know that you will pause periodically to take questions—and then be sure to do so.

Don't forget to prepare a good description of the upcoming call that explains the benefits to the customer. For example, if you're offering a teleseminar called "Get Started in the Pastry Business," your copy could look something like this:

Get Started in the Pastry Business with Bob the Baker

Listeners will discover:

- How to get started for less than $500
- Where to locate no-cost and low-cost commercial kitchen space
- The top five recipes you must add to your collection
- The top five recipes to avoid
- Secrets to profitability in three months or less
- How to locate suppliers and receive hefty discounts

- Low-cost marketing solutions
- Twelve steps to starting your business by next weekend

Notice how the bullet points not only are enticing, but promise to answer important questions about the pastry business. The description generates enthusiasm and tells the potential listener exactly what to expect. Always make sure to deliver on your promises.

In addition to preparing a teleseminar topic, you also need a way to collect payment and register customers. This is where a shopping cart service such as Paypal or 1ShoppingCart will come in handy. Once users pay for the call, you can then send them the dial-in access code and any relevant instructions for participation.

You will need to use a conference call service provider to conduct your call. Many offer free conference call services but provide the callers with a long distance number. Since so many people use cell phones, which typically don't charge for long distance, this is usually not a problem. If you want to provide a toll-free number, you will need to factor the additional costs into the price of your call.

The service provider should also offer the ability to record the call. If you choose to record your calls, you can then have the recordings copied to tapes or CDs, made available for immediate download, or transcribed to print format. Each of these formats can enhance your product line as new revenue generators.

TELECONFERENCE SERVICE PROVIDERS

- ✔ Great Teleseminars: www.greatteleseminars.com
- ✔ Free Conference Call: www.freeconferencecall.com
- ✔ Conference Call.com: www.conferencecall.com
- ✔ Budget Conferencing: www.budgetconferencing.com
- ✔ Audio Acrobat (recording technology): www.audioacrobat.com

Before you launch your teleseminar, it's a good idea to plan out your time. The information should flow in a logical order. Try writing a rough script of the call so you can stick to a time line and avoid omitting important information.

You will want to open with a welcome to your listeners as well as a brief introduction of yourself and any guests. Be sure to offer guidelines for the call, such as etiquette tips and details on how participants can mute their phones. Next, make a list of topics or questions you plan to cover. You might also want to make notes of the points you want to discuss with each topic. Decide at what point you will open the call to questions. Develop a closing paragraph or two to thank listeners for participating and to let them know where to get additional information. This is a good time to remind listeners about your web site link as well as your guest's web site. Your teleseminar should cover the 12 points in the following outline:

Sample Teleconference Process Outline

1. Welcome listeners.
2. Introduce yourself.
3. Introduce guest.
4. Read guest bio (150 words or so).
5. State ground rules for the call (let callers know they will be muted until you open the line for questions).
6. Provide a topic overview ("Today we're going to discuss . . .").
7. Call content script (have a list of questions or topic outline prepared).
8. Open the call for questions (if and when appropriate).
9. Keep an eye on the time (if you're paying for a service, it could cost you more if you go over an hour).
10. Wrap up the call.
11. Tell listeners where to get additional information (your web site and guest's web site).
12. Thank listeners and the guest.

It's a good idea to practice your delivery prior to your first live call. You might consider enlisting friends or family to help you with a mock call. Once you feel confident with your materials, you should be ready to meet your audience. Remember to make it fun and inject some personality into the event.

To entice attendees, you may also want to offer a handout with registration. You can easily provide a downloadable document as a bonus either before or after the call, or give away one of your existing eBooks or special reports.

AUDIO AND VIDEO PRODUCTS

Video, cassette, and CD recordings can command big bucks for topics that are in high demand. Leading industry experts, such as Mark Victor Hansen and Dottie Walters, sell recordings of their programs for several hundred dollars. This is an excellent option for professional speakers or trainers since you can (and should) record every speaking engagement and earn residual income from it for years.

If you are speaking at a large event, ask the event planner if he or she will be recording or videotaping your presentation. You may be able to work with the recording company that has already contracted to be there and purchase the master copy of your presentation. This option should be written into your contract with the event host. The event host may also ask for the right to resell your recordings, so be prepared to negotiate this option.

Recording events where you are already speaking is the most natural way to develop audio and video products. You can also produce your own event to create an audio or video program; just be sure to make it as authentic as possible. Without a live audience, you will not be able to gauge the audience reaction—nor will it be evident in the recording. You can check your local phone book to find video production services. Prices and production quality can vary greatly, so ask for some samples and get several quotes.

If you're interested in videotaping a demonstration, a live audience may not be necessary. Another option is to invite a small audience to give the program some depth. Be sure to script out your presentation in advance, just as you would with any speaking engagement.

The key to success with audio and video products is to maintain high quality while generating market demand. Products should be professionally edited and packaged. While burning CDs or DVDs on your home computer is relatively easy, you will want to use the services of a professional production company if your goal is to make real money from your offerings.

Because of the work involved, professional production will also require a more significant financial investment. The flip side is that people expect to pay more for audio and video products. The good news is that because of the proliferation of companies that compete in this industry, the prices for these services have become more affordable.

RESOURCES FOR AUDIO AND VIDEO PRODUCTION

- ✔ Cassette Works offers duplication of audio and video products: www.m2com.com/cassetteworks.html
- ✔ VCorp also offers duplication services: www.vcorp99.com
- ✔ Video Project Studio offers full-service video production: www.videoprojectstudio.com
- ✔ Fed Ex/Kinkos offers CD and DVD duplication services: www .fedex.com/us/officeprint/main

SEMINARS, WORKSHOPS, AND WORKBOOKS

Seminars and workshops can be a tremendous source of revenue, though they also require a lot of preparation. To achieve success with these products, you need to have access to a broad potential audience.

People like Mark Victor Hansen command up to $1,000 in registration fees from seminar attendees, and then upsell their products throughout the event. In many cases, the product sales can be just as lucrative, or even more lucrative, than attendance fees.

Most major seminars are conducted at hotels or conference centers. These venues have experience coordinating events and can provide everything from refreshments to microphones and display tables. Most charge rental fees for rooms and equipment, as well as a fee per person for food and beverage services. All will require a deposit to schedule a date on their books.

The big seminar companies invest thousands of dollars in promoting their events with direct mail. If you have a substantial mailing list, you may be able to fill your own seminar. Another option is to form an alliance with another business owner or several business owners. Together, you can share mailing lists, costs, and resources to create a mammoth event. You could also offer an affiliate fee for those who help you promote the event—and make the fee attractive enough to be worth their while.

PLANNING AN EVENT

To get started with your own seminar, contact local hotels and seminar venues and begin comparing rates. Give yourself plenty of time (several months) for planning and promotion. Don't forget to develop a marketing plan and follow through by getting as much publicity as possible.

In addition to your books or audio programs, you may want to create a workbook for participants to complete either during or after your presentation. A workbook can complement virtually any kind of presentation. These can simply consist of copied pages loaded in a binder or you could opt to have them professionally bound at your local copy shop or from a company such as BookLocker.com or Lulu.com. Workbooks have a high perceived value that can equate to a higher retail price (think $24.95 and up).

In general, back-of-the-room sales should be part of any presentation you give. This is where many professional speakers make the bulk of their income. Be sure to be prepared by bringing along or shipping in advance— plenty of your information products. Ideally, you want to enlist the help of someone (spouse, assistant, etc.) to collect payments for you. Make sure you bring the following with you:

- ✔ **A tablecloth:** Don't count on the venue to provide one. This is a simple way to enhance the appearance of your display.
- ✔ **A locking cash box with plenty of change:** If you round your prices up to even numbers and include sales tax in each item's price, you won't have to fool with odd amounts of change.
- ✔ **A credit card imprinting machine:** You should already have a merchant account with Internet access, but if the venue doesn't have Internet access (which is highly unusual these days) you will need a manual credit card swiping device and credit card slips. You can purchase these from your processor or through eBay. These are also good to have on hand just in case something goes awry with your processor.

✔ **An attractive sign:** Contact your local signage companies to compare costs of a simple sign that you can either prop up on the table or display from a banner holder. Your local copy shop can also create poster-size signs for less than $100.

✔ **Marketing materials and business cards:** Have plenty of these on hand to remind attendees where to find you later.

✔ **Handouts for attendees:** Give your attendees something to keep as a memento of your presentation. Whether it be a list of tips, a brochure of ideas, a list of resources, or an article—provide them with something tangible to remember you by. Better yet, give them something of value that they will actually want to use long after your presentation is over. This is your chance to create a fan for life.

Be careful not to turn your presentations into sales pitches. If attendees like what you have to say, they will naturally be interested in your products. At the end of your discussion, simply invite them back to your "autograph table."

OTHER PEOPLE'S SEMINARS

If the idea of speaking at seminars and events appeals to you, but you aren't ready to host your own events, you still have plenty of options:

✔ Become a professional speaker. Start by speaking for free at events to build up your experience. Make sure to ask for a testimonial from each event sponsor and reprint these in your marketing materials. Eventually, you will be able to charge for your speaking services. Major keynote speakers receive upward of $10,000 in speaking fees, and the event sponsor pays all their travel expenses. It may take several years, but you could certainly work your way up to the keynote level.

✔ Teach classes at the Learning Annex. With learning centers in major cities all over the country, there are many options for those interested in teaching. Visit www.learningannex.com for details.

✔ Teach classes at your local adult learning center or college. These venues are always looking for new instructors.

✔ Contact your peers and strategic business partners. Let them know you are available to speak at their events.

✔ Contact your local chamber of commerce and offer to present at their meetings.

✔ Contact any trade associations where you are a member. Not only could you offer to speak for them, but they may also maintain a directory of members who are speakers and could give you leads for speaking engagements.

✔ If you live near a major events center, visit the venue's web site to view the calendar of upcoming events. If there are events that match your interests, contact the event planner to inquire about speaking.

✔ For more speakers' resources, including links to speakers' associations and industry information, visit www.businessinfoguide.com /speaking.htm. Also, refer back to Chapter 2, where professional speaking is discussed at length.

ELECTRONIC CLASSES

Joe Vitale has famously told his story about how he sold e-mail classes to earn enough money to buy his dream car. It was a BMW Roadster that provided the inspiration for him to increase his earnings potential. Once he got his heart set on the car, he was compelled to find a way to buy it.

At the time he had an e-mail list of just 600 people. He decided to offer an e-mail course on spiritual marketing and charge each student $1,500. He planned to send out a weekly instructional message along with homework that the students would return for his personal feedback. Fifteen people enrolled in his first class, and his subsequent classes were met with the same or better response.

Though his price point was steep, Vitale had the audience and the topic that made it work. Whether you want to charge $29 or $2,900 for an e-learning course, several options are available.

You can:

✔ Host live web-based seminars (videoconferencing) using technologies provided by WebEx (www.webex.com), Lifesize (www.lifesize .com), or other web conferencing service providers.

✔ Deliver classes via e-mail on a daily or weekly basis.

✔ Set up autoresponders and automate the use of e-mail to teach classes.

✔ Set up a forum where students can interact and exchange information. See www.phpbb.com or www.phorum.org.

✔ Use computer-based training (CBT) software to deliver sophisticated online training classes. See www.customguide.com, www.trigent.com, or www.epathlearning.com.

✔ Host a live teleseminar.

✔ Sell course materials including any type of information product: workbook, printed book, eBook, audio program, or other product. You can offer these for an additional fee or include them as a special bonus for registering for your course.

Although it may seem relatively simple to implement a cyber training program, be careful not to take it too lightly. As with all the products that you create and sell, you want to make sure your offering is of the highest quality possible. Your course content should focus on the needs of the students. Spend time planning out your curriculum before you launch your venture. Decide whether you want to receive and manage homework and how you want to interact with students.

TIPS BOOKLETS

Printed tips booklets can be sold individually, in quantities, or licensed for reprint by other businesses. A tips booklet typically includes a list of topics such as "50 Ways to Improve Your Health" or "100 Tips for Busy Parents."

Paulette Ensign is the founder of www.tipsbooklets.com. Her first booklet, "110 Ideas for Organizing Your Busy Life," has sold almost a million copies through distribution agreements she has formed with businesses. She uses her booklets to gain media exposure and has built a lucrative business around the entire process.

There are plenty of opportunities for maximizing tips booklets:

✔ Individual product sales

✔ Bulk orders and licensing agreements (the right to reprint)

✔ Bonus giveaways with other product purchases

✔ Handouts for seminars and speaking engagements

✔ Samples that you can send to the media

Booklets can be simple black and white, full color, or printed with a color cover. Keep in mind that any use of color will drive the cost up substantially. Your local copy shop can print and bind booklets for you. For substantial quantities, you should request quotes from various printing companies in your area to make sure you get the best price possible. Another option is to let the buyer handle the reprinting costs and simply sell the license.

SUBSCRIPTION NEWSLETTERS

Every business owner should be sending out a free newsletter or e-zine to market his or her services, but many infopreneurs generate income from subscription newsletters in addition to offering free newsletters.

✔ Joan Stewart sells an 8-page bimonthly newsletter delivered in PDF format via e-mail for $49.95 per year (www.publicityhound.com).

✔ Barbara Winter sells her bimonthly newsletter and mails it to subscribers for $36.00 per year (www.barbarawinter.com).

✔ Denise O'Berry sells her 8-page monthly newsletter delivered in PDF format via e-mail for $9.00 per month (www.deniseoberry .com).

✔ Dottie Walters took it a step further and publishes a quarterly print magazine for $100.00 for a two-year subscription (www .speakandgrowrich.com).

Subscription sales can generate excellent ongoing revenue, but newsletters also require a fair amount of work. To maintain a happy customer base, the content needs to be fresh, the quality needs to be top-notch, and the delivery needs to be consistent.

When planning to create a money-making newsletter, be sure you can come up with enough topics and content to make it interesting. Consider how a magazine is organized. There are a variety of sections that have a special focus. This may be a good way to lay the foundation for your publication.

Several infopreneurs that offer these kinds of subscriptions also offer bonus products. Dottie Walters gives away a copy of her *International Directory of Speaker's Bureaus* and a two-CD album to each new subscriber to her magazine. She also sells advertising, which can quickly increase the profit margin.

If you decide to deliver your publication via e-mail, you can either insert the text directly into the e-mail message, provide a link to read the content online, or deliver your publication in PDF format. For printed newsletters, Microsoft Publisher offers preformatted templates for newsletter design that can easily be customized to suit your needs.

Print publications will require printing services. It is probably most cost effective to compare the prices of printing companies in your area. You can expect to negotiate price breaks when you commit to long-term contracts. Also check with the post office for bulk mailing rates.

PRICING STRATEGIES

Assigning a price to your products can be daunting since existing products in the marketplace have a wide variety of pricing structures. In the retail world, pricing is relatively simple. You take the wholesale cost of a product and double it. But in the world of selling information, the rules aren't always as clear.

You will want to factor in your costs, which can be significantly higher for physical products (books, audio programs, CDs, etc.) while leaving enough room to make a profit. If you have been reading the infopreneur profiles in this book, you can already see a vast array of pricing strategies. Many infopreneurs begin by pricing their products on the lower end of the scale and then ramp them up over time. This can be a good way to gauge the market interest in your products. Joan Stewart noted in her interview (see Chapter 1) that she was worried about raising the price of her special reports from $7 to $9; but when she made the move, she saw no reduction in sales.

Some infopreneurs price their products at the higher end of the scale to create a higher perceived value. When comparing products side by side, the one with the higher price may seem more attractive simply because of the price. For example, if you were going to celebrate a special occasion with a nice steak dinner, would you prefer the $9.95 buffet special or the $29.95 meal from the fancy steakhouse? If quality is important to you, you will likely choose the more expensive meal. But beware; if you charge the higher price, make sure your product meets the increased expectations of your buyers.

Your pricing strategy should factor in many variables: how much competition you have and what it is charging for comparable products, costs for production and delivery, the size of your audience, the uniqueness of your offerings, how much commission you want to offer your affiliates, and the overall demand for your products.

Spend some time researching the products in your market before you make your decision. If you truly have a niche offering with little or no competition, you may be able to aim high from the get-go. Whether you start high or low, you can always adjust your prices to see how the demand changes.

ORDER FULFILLMENT

If you decide to sell physical products such as CDs, books, or tips booklets, you will need to devise a system for product delivery. This requires that you designate a space in your home or office to safely store your products and shipping materials. Make sure the space you designate is clean and organized. You don't want to have a hard time locating products or lose track of the inventory you have available. Climate control is another important consideration. Humidity can do awful things to books so the garage and basement are probably poor choices for warehouse space.

Shipping materials can be expensive unless you order them in bulk. Some shipping services provide envelopes and boxes for free. Compare rates and services offered by the U.S. Post Office (www.usps.gov), United Parcel Service (www.ups.com), Federal Express (www.fedex.com), and other shipping providers to determine which will best meet your needs.

If you decide you need to purchase padded mailers or boxes for shipping, several providers are available. Your local office supply store is probably the most expensive option, unless you can speak with the management about purchasing supplies in bulk for a discount. Some suppliers to consider are www.uline.com and www.papermart.com. Don't forget to check eBay. The cost of shipping supplies has become quite competitive online and some good deals can be found on eBay.

It's a good idea to include additional marketing materials with any orders that you ship. If you've ever purchased anything online, you know that the major retailers, such as Amazon.com, always include marketing materials inside their packages. Here are some ideas for items to include:

- ✔ Brochure of your services and products
- ✔ Order form to purchase additional products
- ✔ Special one-time offer with discount off a specific product or products
- ✔ Business card
- ✔ Rolodex card
- ✔ Complete catalog of product offerings
- ✔ Sample newsletter
- ✔ Tips sheet or booklet
- ✔ Bookmark with details about your book
- ✔ Postcard—either blank or to be used to request more information
- ✔ Invitation to visit your web site
- ✔ List of upcoming events
- ✔ Coupons or ads for other businesses (you can earn some revenue from these)

Don't miss this valuable opportunity to up-sell your products and educate your customers on other offers from your business. It is also a nice touch to include a personal note of thanks to the buyer.

If you find that storing and shipping your own products is too labor intensive, then you might want to consider contracting with an order fulfillment service. Services like these will stock your products and handle packaging and shipping. These services come with a significant price tag, but if your business is busy enough to demand it, it could be worth the expense. Be sure to check your local phone book to see if there is a service provider near you. If not, use our list to begin investigating your options.

FULFILLMENT SERVICE PROVIDERS

- ✔ Small Business Warehousing: www.sbwarehousing.com
- ✔ Ship SMO: www.shipsmo.com
- ✔ Specialty Fulfillment Center: www.pickandship.com

Infopreneur Profile

Tom Antion
Antion & Associates
Virginia Beach, Virginia
www.antion.com

PUBLICATIONS:

We have an enormous number of info products including a self-published book; a major publisher book; audio CD albums; single and double audio albums; 15 eBooks in PDF, Palm, and Microsoft Reader formats; DVDs; videos; mentor programs; teleseminars; and speeches. Here is a sampling:

- *The Ultimate Guide to Electronic Marketing for Small Business* (trade paperback, John Wiley & Sons, $19.95)
- *Click: The Ultimate Guide to Electronic Marketing for Speakers* (eBook, $97.00)
- *How to Become a Professional Speaker* (audiotape, $19.95)
- *How to Sell a Ton at the Back of the Room* (audiotape or CD, $39.95)
- *Wake 'Em Up! Business Presentations* (eBook $19.95, trade paperback $24.95)

Who is your target audience for your materials?
Speakers, authors, coaches, consultants, small business owners.

Where do you sell your materials?
Various web sites that I own, affiliate sales, catalog companies, Amazon, Barnes and Noble, Books-A-Million and other places that sell info products.

When did you first publish your material?
I've been doing this since about 1988.

How did your journey to become an infopreneur begin?
I've always had an easy time writing "How to" info. The reason I got into it was because every time I would get some type of skill under my belt other people would ask me to teach them the skill. In many cases writing down and illustrating the instructions kept me from repeating myself over and

over. Soon people were offering to pay me for my how-to information. Then I started putting the same information in three-ring binders and on video, which got even more money for the information I was able to generate. I've been doing it ever since and have sold many millions of dollars worth of information products and speeches.

What made you decide to self-publish?
Speed to market, total control of the project, and maximum financial returns.

How did you secure your book deal with a major publisher?
A publisher approached me after reviewing one of my eBooks. I did not solicit that publisher's interest in any way.

How does publication enhance your business?
Although books are the lowest return and most hassle product to create, they do position you as an expert and are a good vehicle for traditional publicity. Once you are positioned as the expert in a field, you have people calling you to do business and your fees rise considerably.

How do your information products enhance your business?
They bring in enormous amounts of revenue without doing extra work. Once I create the product, it can sell for me over and over again.

How do you market your materials? What marketing strategies have and haven't worked?
I'm almost exclusively Internet based. I sell in 40 countries around the world through my electronic magazine and good search engine placement. I also am one of the top back-of-the-room sales speakers in the industry.

What has been the most challenging part of the publishing process?
So far DVD production is still too hard to easily do at your desktop. Other than that, it is easier than ever to produce quality info products.

What has been the most rewarding part of the publishing process?
I like the money.

What have you learned from the experience that you would like to share with others?
People are lazy and will pay you lots of money to figure something out for them and tell them how to do it.

Looking back, is there anything you would do differently?
I would have started even sooner than I did. I thought it was too hard to create products and then when I found out how easy it was, I was kicking myself for not learning how to do it sooner.

Is there anything else you would like to add to this profile?
Everyone has knowledge or can learn and compile knowledge that someone else will pay for. It's a great way to make a living—I mean make a fantastic living that can make you more wealthy than you ever imagined.

Your Web Site: Build It and They Will Come

Opportunity is missed by most people because it is dressed in overalls and looks like work.

—THOMAS A. EDISON

If I had to pick one secret to success with information products, it would be having an excellent web site. It doesn't matter what business you are in—if you're a sheep farmer or an origami guru—you need a web site. Not only does a web site add credibility to your business, but it lets you reach a potential customer base across the globe. It is inexpensive to host a web site and can be worth every penny.

I have three web sites and own a dozen domain names that are marked for future projects. Each web site serves a unique purpose:

1. **www.stephaniechandler.com:** This is my author web site. I use it to promote my writing, especially with editors. I post sample clips of my published articles so editors can see my experience. I receive messages through this site from people who have read an article or one of my books. The site was selected by

Writer's Digest magazine as one of the 10 best writer's web sites in 2005.

2. **www.bookloverscafe.com:** I own a brick-and-mortar bookstore in Sacramento, California, and the main purpose for this site is to attract new customers. I have optimized it with the search engines (more on how to do this later in this chapter) so that customers find the site easily when searching for bookstores in Sacramento. I also use it as a venue for communicating with customers and promoting in-store events. The media references the site whenever someone covers us in a story. It is an essential tool to my brick and mortar business.

3. **www.businessinfoguide.com:** This site is the core of my infopreneur business. It is a content-rich site that attracts my core audience: entrepreneurs. By providing plenty of free information, I am able to build a relationship with site visitors. I send a monthly newsletter and strive to offer useful information that makes people look forward to receiving my newsletter. As a result, my information products sell while I sleep. It's a wonderful thing! And the best part is that I can sleep easy because I know I am providing quality information for a reasonable price. If you visit this site, you should see the formula for info product success:

Information + Marketing = Sales

It's that simple.

Figure out what kind of information your customers need and make it available on your web site. You already have a built-in customer base and all you need to do is produce a quality product and convince them to get their wallets out. Make your products available on your web site and with the right marketing copy, you'll be on your way.

DOMAIN SEARCH AND WEB SITE SETUP

If you are starting a new business, before you settle on your business name, make sure the domain name is available. The Internet continues to grow rapidly and many domain names with a ".com" extension are already taken. You can use ".net" or ".biz," but consider the ramifications of doing so. If a potential client types in www.yourbusiness.com by accident, will they find your competition?

To check if your domain is available, you can run a free search at http://smallbusiness.yahoo.com. If the domain is not available, consider using an acronym or abbreviation. If the name is available and you are not yet ready to commit to hosting a web site, you may want to invest in registering the domain name. It costs less than $10 and gives you ownership of the name for one year, which you can later activate and convert into an active web site. When you register your domain name with Yahoo! you can also create a single-page business card with your contact information. You can keep this active until you are ready to make your web site live.

If the web site name you want is not available, type it into your browser to see if it is active. If not, you can check the ownership information and expiration date of the current ownership by visiting www.internic .net/whois.html. If you have time, you may want to wait for the registration to expire to see if the name becomes available, or contact the owner to see if he is willing to transfer the rights to you for a reasonable fee.

There is also a web-hosting service that, for a fee, will track a domain name until it becomes available and then will attempt to register it for you. They cannot guarantee that they can get the domain name, but if it's one you want badly enough, it might be worth the price. Visit www.godaddy .com for details.

Many free web sites are available from places like Geocities (http://geocities.yahoo.com). Just keep in mind that you will not have your own domain name or e-mail address. Instead your URL will look something like this: www.geocities.com/yourbusiness.html. If you want to establish a professional presence on the Internet, you should consider an affordable web site hosting plan and your own domain name.

You can host your own web site for as little as $12 per month with Yahoo! at www.smallbusiness.yahoo.com. Their starter package includes hosting and up to 25 e-mail accounts that you can set up however you like. For example, you can have yourname@yourweb site.com, webmaster@yourweb site.com, customerservice@yourweb site.com, and so on.

Another advantage of using Yahoo! is that you can upgrade to a Yahoo! storefront if you decide to sell products. Yahoo! also offers free site-building tools and templates that make the process relatively easy for a simple web site operation.

If Yahoo! isn't for you, there are plenty of other options. Be sure to investigate the contracts with any hosting provider that you consider. You want to make sure that the domain is transferable in case you decide to switch service providers later on. You also want a guarantee of site availability and data protection. This is especially important if your web site generates income or plays a substantial role in your business.

Nothing can hurt an online business more than downtime. If your site is down, you are effectively out of business until it is up and running again, and you could potentially lose customers. Make sure that your hosting provider performs regular data backups and guarantees availability. Some of the smaller hosting providers may not even back up your data, which means that if their web servers crash, you will be responsible for restoring your site. I've heard plenty of horror stories from people who have hosted with small providers that offered no guarantee of site availability and ended up with days and weeks of downtime and a painful process of getting the web site up and running again.

For other hosting options, Network Solutions (www.NetworkSolutions .com) has a small business start-up package for $35 per year that includes hosting and one e-mail address. The downside of having only one e-mail address is that you can't set up multiple mailboxes for customer service, sales, questions, and so on. GoDaddy.com (www.godaddy.com) offers hosting for as little as $3.95 per month. Just be sure to weigh the value of less expensive hosting since some of these services charge for extras such as web site security and traffic data (which you will want to have). A package that includes these options may be most cost effective.

SITE DESIGN SECRETS

There are scores of options for web site design. You can do it yourself or get someone to do it for you. It really depends on your needs and your skill set. I've tried several methods, with varied results.

The most important priority is to make sure your web site looks professional. Would you buy a product from a clunky site that was full of grammatical errors or looked as if it had been designed by a child? Whatever you decide to do, make sure your site is visually appealing, the content is edited, and the information is organized. The good news is that you don't have to be a professional web site designer to get professional results.

I initially designed the bookstore web site (www.bookloverscafe .com) after teaching myself how to use Microsoft Frontpage. It was a good idea to learn to use Frontpage since I now manage two of my sites with it and love the control and flexibility of the product. But my design skills are awful! So when a web site designer came along and offered to redesign it for me (we bartered with bookstore services), I jumped at the opportunity. She put the site in a nice clean format and handed over the files for me to manage.

What I liked most about this arrangement was the time I saved because I only had to provide the content and feedback on how things were developing. Overall it was a good experience. But since then I've learned a few tricks.

Several months later, I decided to launch my author web site (www.stephaniechandler.com). Since I knew my design skills were lacking and I knew I only needed a simple static site, I looked to my hosting provider for help. I used Yahoo's free Site Builder tool and one of their preformatted templates. The tool is user-friendly, and I got the web site up and running in just one evening. I continue to use the tool for site management since the site is not complicated and doesn't require frequent updates.

The big revelation came when I designed my business web site (www.businessinfoguide.com). This was when I discovered web site templates. For around $20, I purchased a preformatted template for use with Frontpage. All the foundation was there, including slick drop-down menus and a professional-looking theme. All I had to do was fill in the content, make a few tweaks, and I was up and running. It was the best $20 I've ever spent. Numerous businesses offer web site templates. I found mine at www.thetemplatestore.com and couldn't be happier with the choice I made.

If you need help with web site design, you have endless options. You may want to ask business owners that you know or those who have web sites that you admire, for a referral to a local web designer. There are plenty of students who can do the job inexpensively, but they may lack enough experience to build an effective site. A professional web site designer should infuse your pages with the right key words and optimize your site to make it easier for search engines to find you. Be sure to ask potential designers if they know how to do this.

If your site mainly serves as an electronic business card with a lot of static data (which is perfectly fine for many types of businesses), then hiring a designer or using a template provided by your hosting provider should be an effective solution for you. If you have some technical skills or want to have the power to change your web site contents frequently, it may be worth your time to learn how to use one of the major web design tools like Microsoft Frontpage or Dreamweaver.

There is a learning curve with both of these tools because they are powerful, but you can take a class at your local college or adult learning center to become proficient. I find that I can almost always find an answer to my questions through online help. The Frontpage Resource site offers all kinds of tips, tutorials, and tricks if you get stuck: http://accessfp.net.

SHOPPING CARTS AND CREDIT CARDS

If you plan to sell products on your web site, you will need to set up a shopping cart and the ability to accept credit cards. Dozens of shopping cart programs are available depending on your needs. You can search the Internet for shopping cart software or use one of the vendors listed here.

If your needs are basic, then Yahoo! merchant solutions (http://smallbusiness.yahoo.com/merchant) may be a good choice. Yahoo! offers a shopping cart starter package for under $40 per month that includes web site hosting, up to 100 e-mail accounts and all the tools to set up your shopping cart. They charge a 1.5 percent transaction fee for each sale under this package.

Yahoo's standard package costs about $100 per month plus a 1 percent transaction fee. The added features include the ability to offer coupons, sales, and gift certificates. All of Yahoo's packages have the option to have your site listed in the Yahoo! Shopping directory.

To accept credit cards with Yahoo!, you can apply for a merchant account with their partner, Paymentech (www.paymentech.net), search for your own merchant account service, or set up an existing merchant account. Paymentech charges a transaction fee of $0.20 plus 2.69 percent along with a monthly fee of $22.95.

Paypal (http://paypal.com) offers a free shopping cart setup on your existing web site and allows you to process your transactions with their credit card payment system. There is no additional transaction fee other than the one used for credit card transactions. The rates for credit card transactions are based on the amount of transactions processed each month. For up to $3,000 in sales, the rate is currently $0.30 per transaction plus a 2.9 percent transaction fee. For $3,000.01 to $10,000 in sales, the rate is $0.30 per transaction plus a 2.5 percent transaction fee. PayPal's shopping cart solution is quick and easy to implement and should work well if you are selling just a few products through your site.

For a complete solution, check out 1ShoppingCart.com (www .1shoppingcart.com). This company offers shopping cart solutions, merchant card processing, autoresponders for e-mail management, and the ability to set up your own affiliate program (you can offer others a commission for sending you product sales). While you can purchase all these services individually from different providers, you would then have to integrate them and manage them all separately.

With 1ShoppingCart.com, you have the whole suite of solutions available. The basic shopping cart costs just $29 per month. The autoresponder package is also $29 per month. Autoresponders let you automate your e-mail responses. For example, if a customer subscribes to your newsletter, an autoresponder can send a thank-you message. You can also set up your autoresponder to send your newsletter or messages to your customers at intervals defined by you. An autoresponder system can be an invaluable tool for an active web site.

For a bundling of the shopping cart and autoresponder services, 1ShoppingCart.com charges $49 per month. For a full-service solution that even allows you to set sale prices on your products and create your own affiliate program, you can purchase the Pro package for $79 per month. The Pro package also allows you to send eBooks and electronic documents to your customers automatically.

WEB SITE CONTENT

There's not much use for a web site that doesn't offer valuable content. Before you even think about launching your site, you need to have a plan to make its content valuable.

The most important consideration is your customer. Start by identifying the target audience for your site. If you want to sell to moms, then your content needs to appeal to moms. If you are targeting students, make it appealing to students.

Every web site is unique, which is part of the intrigue of the World Wide Web. But all sites should have some basic information. Include the following on your site:

✔ **About Us:** This page describes your business, the people involved in the company, and gives the company history. It can be formal or friendly, depending on the overall tone of your web site.

✔ **Contact Us:** In addition to an e-mail address, you should also list a mailing address and phone number on your web site. Every legitimate business needs a way for customers to contact them, even if you list your cell phone number. And don't worry too much about getting overwhelmed with sales calls. Thanks to the crackdown on telemarketers, if you're on a Do Not Call list, you shouldn't see your calls increase simply because your number is publicly available. If you operate from home, you will want to get a post office box. It just makes good sense to avoid publishing your home address.

✔ **Privacy Policy:** This can be its own page or listed on the About Us page. Be sure to reassure your customers that you will not share their information—and follow through on your promise! Nobody likes a spammer and if you share contacts without customers' permission, your reputation will deteriorate faster than a banana rotting in the sun.

✔ **Subscribe Here:** You should be sending an e-zine on a monthly basis at a minimum. This is a great cost-effective way to engage your customers and keep your name in front of them. Make it easy to subscribe by placing a link or subscription form on every page of your site. Start gathering contact information as soon as your site is live and send a newsletter consistently, even if you only have two subscribers. It's also a good idea to publish a sample of a previous e-zine. See Chapter 9 for more information on publishing an e-zine/newsletter.

✔ **Disclaimer:** Make sure you limit your liability with site visitors by including a disclaimer on your About Us page. Check your statement with your lawyer to make sure it includes all the necessary terminology.

As for the rest of your content, the possibilities are endless. The keyword in this paragraph is content—you want to give your visitors lots of it. Not only are you providing value, but the more content you offer, the better your chances of being found through Internet searches.

The following are additional types of content to consider:

✔ **Links:** While you don't want to give your site visitors a reason to leave your site, you do want to give them a reason to visit your site. Offer valuable resources by including links to other sites related to your industry. Be sure to make the links open in a new window so your visitor doesn't go away completely. BusinessInfoGuide.com is built on links to business start-up resources, and this strategy has worked well. This is also a great way to build up reciprocal links since you can offer to link-swap with other sites that you admire.

Be careful that your site does not become a link farm. Many sites are started by farming links to attract visitors. There is little quality or thought put into this—and that's the last thing you should do. Avoid endorsing any site that you aren't at least somewhat familiar with.

✔ **Articles:** As an information provider, not only do you want to sell information, but you should give some away, too. You can write your own articles and also publish articles by other people. Look to your peers for content or visit free content sites to find quality articles that relate to your business. Good sites to visit include www.ezinearticles.com, www.ideamarketers.com, and www.articlealley.com.

✔ **Free Stuff:** Everyone loves getting free stuff. Have you ever wondered why celebrities are given free designer dresses and merchandise? The suppliers do that in hopes that the celebrity will talk about their products. And even though celebrities have plenty of money, they still love to get stuff for free. Use this concept to make your site visitors happy. Offer a free eBook or special report as a thank-you for subscribing to your newsletter. Remember, you are building a relationship with your site visitors. If they like the quality of the free information you are providing, they are more likely to invest in your products.

✔ **Media Info:** If you want your business to be big, you have to think big. Contacting the media on a regular basis is an excellent way to build exposure for your business. Make it easy for them by including your recent press releases on your site. Include the kind of information found in a press kit, including a company history, high-quality photographs, and any other details the media could use for developing a story about you.

SEARCH ENGINE OPTIMIZATION

Entire books have been written on the subject of search engine optimization, also commonly known as SEO. Search engine optimization is what you do to improve your rankings with the search engines. So when someone searches for "Free Kittens," the search engine lists the results based on a variety of factors for each web site that contains the search term.

To complicate matters further, each search engine has different criteria for how it ranks web pages—and the criteria keep changing. Google has complex algorithms that it uses, although the company has been open about sharing the details. You can visit Google's site, or any of the search engines, to find their latest suggestions for optimizing your site. For now, I'll share with you some basics that you should be doing at a minimum.

Titles, Keywords, and Content

Every web page design tool has a place for you to indicate the page title and keywords. This information gets encoded in the page and is the first data most of the search engines see. Each and every page of your web site should have its own title. The title is displayed at the top of the browser, as well as in the data returned in a search, and as the description when someone bookmarks the page in their Internet Favorites folder. A lot of sites simply read "Home" at the top of the page. Don't make this mistake! Be sure to give a brief description of your web page.

The keywords describe the content on the web page. The web page for my book *The Business Startup Checklist and Planning Guide* has the following keywords: business book, startup checklist, business startup, business startup checklist, startup book, startup manual, advice for, entrepreneur, small business, stephanie chandler, start a business, starting a business, how to start a business.

Keywords only work well if they match the *content* on your web page. So when you're writing your web copy, it's best to repeat important keyword phrases throughout the page. If you want your page to come up when someone searches for "Startup Checklist," then there should be several mentions of startup checklist throughout the text on the page.

There is a caveat to all this. The search engines will penalize you if you try to beat the system. So don't bother repeating keywords dozens of times—they will view this as site manipulation and it could actually hurt your ranking or get you removed from the search engine all together.

And don't forget to include a brief description of each web page. This is the information that is listed when your page shows up in search engine results. Make sure your description includes as many of your keywords as possible without being too long. Most engines will cut off your description after 100 or 150 words.

More about Keywords

Keywords are extremely important in attracting visitors to your site. If you sell pottery, but have no or little mention of the word pottery on your site, it will be more difficult for visitors to find you.

When defining your keywords, think about what your potential site visitors would search for to locate you. Keywords don't have to be single words, they can include phrases. Be sure to figure out what combinations are most likely to attract visitors. Also keep in mind that if you have a highly popular search phrase, such as "Start a Business," you will have a lot of competition to get into the top-ranking positions. And those competitors are paying big bucks to be in the top 10 or 20 listings. Try to include additional keywords that not everyone in your industry is using.

⚡ Hot Tip ⚡

You can view the keywords on virtually any web page simply by viewing it in your browser. This can be very handy in understanding what your competitors are using. To do this with Internet Explorer, display a web page and click on **View → Source.** The HTML source code will display and near the top you will see keywords listed in the text.

SUBMIT TO SEARCH ENGINES

The search engines won't know your web site exists if you don't tell them about it. So once your site is up and running, be sure to submit it to the major search engines. This doesn't cost anything but time. Here are some links to get you started:

✔ **Yahoo:** http://submit.search.yahoo.com/free/request
✔ **Google:** www.google.com/addurl.html
✔ **Google's Froogle Merchant Program:** www.google.com/froogle /merchants/apply
✔ **Open Directory Project:** http://dmoz.org/add.html
✔ **MSN:** http://beta.search.msn.com/docs/submit.aspx
✔ **Addme:** http://tools.addme.com/servlet/s0new
✔ **Subjex:** www.subjex.net/submit_url.html
✔ **Free Web Submission:** www.freewebsubmission.com
✔ **Info Tiger:** www.infotiger.com/addurl.html
✔ **Entireweb:** http://addurl.entireweb.com/main.php
✔ **Nerd World:** www.nerdworld.com/nwadd.html

SITE UPDATES

Believe it or not, you can be penalized by the search engines if you make changes to every page on your web site all at once. It is perfectly fine to update several pages at a time. In fact, new content draws the attention of the search engine "crawlers." But some engines penalize sites that update all their pages at the same time. You can't avoid it if you are making a complete site overhaul. Just be aware that you could drop down a few notches in your positioning and it may take some time to climb up again.

LINKS, LINKS, LINKS

One criterion the engines use to rank web site pages is to look at how many other links are pointing to your pages. More importantly, they look at how many links from high-traffic web sites are pointing to your pages.

This is the reason link swapping is so popular. The theory is that the more links to your web site, the better. Make sure you list your link everywhere possible. Include it in your signature file that you post online. Update the profile for any trade organizations that you belong to. Ask colleagues to swap links with you. It takes time to get your link out there, so develop as many strategies as you can. This is a major benefit of publishing articles online since the more your article is syndicated to other web sites, the more your link is published.

PAID SEARCH ENGINE OPTIMIZATION AND PLACEMENT

There are many opinions on whether optimization is worth the cost. You can subscribe to services that promise to improve your site rankings. If you consider these services, be sure to check references or get a referral from someone you know.

One of the more popular options is paid placement by Overture (www.overture.com). In this case, you actually bid on keywords by indicating how much you are willing to pay for each click-through to your site. Bids can start as low as $0.25 each and popular keyword phrases can cost several dollars for each click depending on how much bidding competition you face. Promoting less-popular keywords might be a good choice for the budget conscious.

Google AdWords (www.google.com) is another option for paid search engine advertising. Google places ads to your site from other sites based on keywords you specify. If you have a pastry business, your ad could be placed on cooking-related sites. With AdWords, you also pay for each click-through to your site.

The challenge with these pay-for-placement services is that you are paying only for a click-through to your site, not when you've actually sold something or gained a new customer. The costs can add up quickly, though many business owners have found ways to make these services work for them. You have the option to set a budget so that if you're only willing to pay $50 per month, these services will pull your ads off after you've reached that amount.

Other Internet companies will submit your site to search engines for you. While you can manually submit to most search engines for free, some services, like those offered by www.SubmitNet.net, offer analyzer tools and web site placement tracking. SubmitNet will notify you when your site ranking is increased. They also have a tool that evaluates the concentration of keywords on each of your web pages, giving you a simple way to analyze your data.

If you have marketing dollars to spend, some of these tools may be a worthwhile investment. Just be careful not to overinvest in a service until you are certain that it's working for you.

TIPS FOR MAXIMIZING ONLINE SALES

Once you have your web site up and running and a shopping cart system in place, the next step is to make sure your web site does its job. It needs to sell your products and services. Don't be shy about promoting your products. Though you should offer enough free content to keep people interested, you also want to make them aware of your products. Here are some tips to get your sales cranking:

- ✔ Make it easy for visitors to find your products. I'm always surprised when I visit a web site that doesn't clearly list a link to a products page. This link should be in the main menu and on every page of your site.

- ✔ Promote each product individually in appropriate places. If you have an eBook about customer service, be sure to provide a link to it after any articles or content pages that discuss customer service. For example, you could simply add a line of text that says, "Want to learn more about customer service? Check out our eBook!" and set up a link to the eBook details page.

- ✔ List all your products on a single page along with links to complete product descriptions.

- ✔ Create a page for each product that includes a comprehensive product description. Include any testimonials for the product and strong sales copy to entice the buyer.

✔ Include a printable order form for people who don't want to place orders online. Give them a way to mail or fax the order to you.

✔ Make sure your purchase process is simple and easy to use. Test it out by purchasing your own products. Are any steps missing? Is the information confusing? Even better, ask a few friends to walk through the process and give you feedback.

✔ Set up a thank-you page. When a customer completes an order with you, make sure they are returned to that page. This page can also be used to up-sell additional products. If someone purchases an eBook, the thank-you page could make a special offer that says, "Readers of our eBook also rave about our audio series. Click here to order our audio collection at 25 percent off!"

✔ Put a "Featured Product" section on your home page or in the sidebar of all your web pages. Change the offer each month to keep it fresh and interesting. You could simply list your selected product or offer it at a discount.

Infopreneur Profile

Alyice Edrich
The Dabbling Mum
Merrill, Wisconsin
www.thedabblingmum.com

PUBLICATIONS:

The following are all available in eBook format with prices ranging from $5.95 to $39.99:

- *Tid-Bits for Making Money with eBooks*
- *Tid-Bits for New [Notary] Signing Agents*
- *Tid-Bits for New Daycare Providers*
- *Tid-Bits for Marketing Your Business with Articles*
- *Mystery Shopping Earns You Perks!*
- *Work-at-Home or Stay-at-Home, You Can Do Both!*

- *The Dabbling Mum Speaks with Successful Authors, Volume 1*
- *Build upon a Firm Foundation: Financial Help with a Biblical Twist*

The following two eBooks were compiled using the works of various authors, in which I purchased the rights to the submissions and now give the books away to new newsletter subscribers (http://thedabblingmum .com/joinezine.htm):

1. *Krack'd Pot Moms Anthology*
2. *Queries & Published Samples*

Brief Description of Contents:

Each of my eBooks give step-by-step processes to running specific businesses. Each of the businesses outlined is a business I've owned and operated firsthand, so I am able to walk readers through the process of starting up such a business and provide valuable resources to help them make the transition to becoming an entrepreneur.

Who is your target audience for your materials?

My target audience includes busy parents who want to own their own businesses—whether it's to make a few extra dollars so they can get out from under debt, or to one day replace their current job.

Where do you sell your materials (your own web site, online directories, Amazon, etc.)?

I sell my eBooks through my own web site. While I do have a couple of eBooks listed on Booklocker.com, I haven't marketed those links in years.

When did your first publish your material?

The first electronic downloadable book I wrote was in 1999 and dealt with working as a notary public. Since that time I've written nine eBooks on topics including marketing your business with articles, writing and selling eBooks, operating a home daycare, and becoming a mystery shopper.

How did your journey to become an infopreneur begin?

Maybe my journey began shortly after I spent hours and hours researching a new career for myself. I heard about an opportunity to make good money as a notary public who specializes in loan document signings, but obtaining professional help in this industry was difficult. There wasn't a class one could take, or a book one could buy, to learn how to do it right, and those who knew the ropes were reluctant to share their information with aspiring notaries for fear of losing part or all of their income.

Then I ran into a few forums where members were sharing just enough information to be helpful but not enough to make it easy for an outsider to get in and learn the business. It was frustrating, to say the least.

I gleaned whatever information I could find from these sites, but eventually I simply had to go out and learn by trial and error. I began keeping notes so that I wouldn't make the same mistake twice. Soon I had a notebook full of information and it seemed like a waste to just keep it to myself, so I compiled the information into a short book and began selling a few copies.

Over time, I fell in love with writing and the ability to change lives through the written word and I naturally drifted toward writing as a full-time career.

What made you decide to self-publish?

I decided to self-publish because I didn't have enough confidence in myself to seek a traditional publisher.

Once I got a taste of being my own publisher there was no turning back. Originally I thought of starting a print magazine, but the overhead and start-up costs weren't something I could afford and definitely not something I wanted to go into debt over. So I began an online magazine and called it the *Dabbling Mum.*

And to be quite frank, another reason I decided to self-publish eBooks is because the profit margin is higher per book.

How does publication enhance your business?

Actually, you can say my business enhances my publications.

The *Dabbling Mum* (http://thedabblingmum.com) is an online magazine with several centers: home business, writing, parenting, and recipes. It's a resource for busy parents who want to find information they can use in their everyday lives.

With a print book, a buyer can walk into a bookstore, browse the pages between the covers, and decide if the book is worth buying. With an eBook, there are no pages to browse. The buyer has to make a choice to trust the author or the publisher and the sales copy they've read.

What was the process you used to publish?

I use Frontpage 2003 and basic html coding to design and maintain my magazine and sales pages. I use Microsoft Word to write my books and I use Adobe to convert them into PDF files. I then use a special shopping cart (http://marketerschoice.com) and a credit card processor (http://paypal.com) to sell my eBooks.

Honestly, it was all by trial and error. While I did read a few books on writing and publishing books with traditional, or print, publishers, there weren't any books on writing and selling eBooks and if there were, I didn't know about them.

At first, I didn't hire an outside editor because I was too afraid of the critique. But a few years later, I met a wonderful woman (http://tinalmiller.com) who really knew her stuff and while she was frank in her assessment of my material, she was also delicate in how she handled the red-lining (or edits). I can honestly say that her edits have made my books stronger.

What other products and services do you sell?

I currently do not have other products or services, but I am hoping to one day expand into audio files and online workshops because there's a huge market for it!

How do you market your materials?

I go into great detail in my book, *Tid-Bits for Making Money with eBooks*, but I'll share some brief tips here:

- I optimize my sales pages for the search engines.
- I write sales pages that match the voice of my magazine.
- I write and distribute articles to other publications and depending on the type of article it is, I request my byline include a mention about my magazine and web address or one of my books and a link to the sales page or a link to http://thedabblinmumpress .com. In fact, when I didn't have the money to pay for advertising, I gave away articles related to my book's topic in exchange for

advertising space and/or an advertorial in my byline. (That's how my book, *Tid-Bits for Marketing Your Business with Articles,* came about.)

- I share valuable information—not sales talk—in appropriate forums and use a tagline for my signature when allowed.
- I place a personal advertisement in each of the weekly newsletters I publish.
- I always accept chances to be interviewed and never mind when the interviewer wants to interview via e-mail instead of the phone.

What has been the most challenging part of the publishing process?

The most challenging part of the publishing process is the juggling act: I have to be the writer, editor, publisher, marketer, distributor, customer service representative, and office staff. Sometimes, I get outside help, but the bulk of the business falls on my lap and it can be exasperating.

What has been the most rewarding part of the publishing process?

The most rewarding part of the publishing process is the freedom to write whatever I want and the personal notes of thanks from readers who genuinely liked the books and felt they've been of value and help. And let's be honest . . . the money!

What have you learned from the experience that you would like to share with others?

I would tell those interested in publishing an eBook that "More is better." If you're planning to write a how-to book, don't leave the reader wondering how you did something. If you are going to mention that you overcame an obstacle, don't just tell us about the obstacle, but tell us how you overcame it. Don't write fluff because fluff is hard to sell.

Looking back, is there anything you would do differently?

I wouldn't be so afraid to ask for help or to interview people for my book.

In the beginning, I was like any new writer. I feared sharing my ideas with others because I thought it would result in people stealing my ideas and coming up with a similar book. While I have had this happen in the past, it is not the norm.

I did have one bad experience when I interviewed one woman who read my questions via e-mail then decided that she wasn't going to answer them. A month later, she released an audio book on that very topic, and it was pretty obvious my interview questions had become the outline for her audio book.

Is there anything else you would like to add to this profile?

Working for ourselves can be harder than working for employers. As an entrepreneur you will put in many unpaid hours before you begin to see a profit and that can leave you wondering if it's all worth it, but if you stick it out and believe in yourself you can make it to the other side—whether it takes one month or two years.

Online Marketing Techniques: Spanning the Globe

Plans are only good intentions unless they immediately degenerate into hard work.

—PETER DRUCKER

With the potential to reach millions of customers around the world, the Internet is a powerful business tool. The opportunities for promoting your business and products are abundant and don't necessarily have to cost a lot of money.

If you can do three to five things every day to market your business, you should see significant results within just a few months. The following are low-cost and no-cost strategies to propel your business success. Not all these strategies are right for every business, so prioritize them to suit your needs and put your marketing plans into action.

SEND A NEWSLETTER OR E-ZINE

This marketing strategy should be used by virtually every type of business. A newsletter creates ongoing communications with your customers and allows you to advertise new products, services, or events. Give readers a reason to read and keep your newsletter by including a special coupon, recipe, or useful article. You can even turn your newsletter into an additional revenue stream by selling advertising space to other businesses.

Sending newsletters through e-mail is virtually free. In most cases, the biggest investment will be in your time. An e-mail newsletter does not need to be flashy but should be easy to read and have valuable content. Minimize the use of graphics because they can make it difficult for some customers to open or even receive your message.

Here are some topic ideas for your newsletter:

- ✔ Brief letter to your customers
- ✔ Calendar of events
- ✔ New product announcement
- ✔ Promotion or sale information
- ✔ A coupon
- ✔ A recipe
- ✔ Articles
- ✔ List of ideas or tips
- ✔ List of resources
- ✔ Highlighting a product
- ✔ Explanation of a product's advantages
- ✔ Quotes from satisfied customers
- ✔ Case studies or customer success stories
- ✔ Advertisements for other businesses
- ✔ Community information

If you don't want to write all the content yourself, you can access free articles on a variety of topics from web sites like IdeaMarketers.com, www.ezinearticles.com, and www.amazines.com. You could also have your employees or even your customers contribute some of the content.

Don't be afraid to promote your products throughout your newsletter. As long as you are providing plenty of useful free content, readers will be glad to know about the opportunity to purchase additional information. For example, if you provide a list of tips for organizing your office, include a link to your eBook on getting organized.

TIPS FOR NEWSLETTER SUCCESS

✔ Encourage new subscribers by making it easy to sign up from every page on your web site.

✔ Figure out what your subscribers want to know and earn their loyalty by delivering valuable content.

✔ Never send unsolicited e-mail. Spammers are running rampant in cyberspace and the quickest way to lose customers is to send unsolicited messages. Make sure you have a privacy policy and stick to it.

✔ Beware of spam filters. The algorithms are changing so fast that it's nearly impossible to keep up, but certain words can stop your messages from getting through. Avoid or modify words like "Free," "Marketing," and "Money." If you need to include words like these you can insert special characters instead: "Fr~ee," "M^rketing," and "M0ney."

✔ Be consistent with delivery. If you promise a weekly e-zine, send it out on the same day each week.

✔ Insert a note encouraging subscribers to "Share this newsletter with a friend!"

✔ To comply with current regulations, you should include a link or instructions for customers to unsubscribe to your newsletter. You shouldn't receive many unsubscribe requests if your content is perceived as valuable.

✔ Remember to include your business contact information, hours of operation, and web site URL in all your correspondence with customers.

Sending the newsletter via e-mail becomes challenging as your list grows larger. If you are using an e-mail program such as Microsoft Outlook or AOL mail, the system may choke when you attempt to send too many messages. Spam filters on the recipients' end may also block a large broadcast from being received by subscribers.

Once your list exceeds 100 subscribers, you should consider investing in a newsletter management system. There are numerous providers to choose from and the fees range from $10 to $100+ per month depending on the number of subscribers you manage and how many broadcasts you send.

These systems allow you to send out mass mailings and create forms on your web site that make it easy for new subscribers to join.

Some providers also offer HTML templates for newsletter design and the ability to set up autoresponders. You can use autoresponders to automate your responses to e-mail or proactively send messages to people on your list. You can set an autoresponder to send a thank-you message to new subscribers. You can set up another autoresponder to send a follow-up message that includes a bonus such as a special report or eBook. If you offer a weekly training class via e-mail, you can set a schedule for an autoresponder to send your messages out at specified intervals. Automating your e-mail management frees up your time to focus on your business and gives you a professional edge over competitors who are attempting to do it all manually.

NEWSLETTER TECHNOLOGY PROVIDERS AND AUTORESPONDERS

- ✔ EZEzine: www.ezezine.com
- ✔ Constant Contact: www.constantcontact.com
- ✔ 1Shopping Cart: www.1shoppingcart.com
- ✔ Zinester: www.zinester.com

⚡ HOT TIP ⚡

It's easy to lose track of what content you've included in past issues of your newsletter. Save time by using a spreadsheet to list the topics, articles, and resources you reference in your newsletter each month. This is a quick and simple way to avoid duplicating content.

PRESS KIT

A press kit is a collection of information and facts that the media can access to learn about your company. In the past, press kits were traditionally delivered by postal mail in hard copy format, but the proliferation of access to the Internet has led to more and more companies making their press kits available online.

Most businesses now offer a link to "Media" or "Press Info" on their web sites. This makes it easy for media professionals to find out more about you if they happen across your site, and you can also send the media links to your online press information. Visit some of your favorite web sites to see how others have compiled their press information. When developing your kit, include enough details that the media not only could write a story based on your information, but would *want* to write about you because the copy is so compelling.

A press kit should provide the following information:

✔ Company history or overview, or your biography if you are the heart of the business

✔ Company officers (if applicable)

✔ Press release archives

✔ Photos of you and your business (high quality)

✔ Previous media coverage (articles, links to media sites, news or radio programs, books you have contributed to, etc.)

✔ Testimonials from others including their contact information (make sure to get their permission first)

✔ One-page fact sheet about your business

✔ Frequently asked questions with answers (written as if conducted as an interview)

✔ Articles you have written

✔ Contact information

There may be times when you will want to send hard copies of your press kit information. In addition to making this information easy to view on a web page, you may also want to offer printable forms on your company letterhead via a PDF download.

TOTALLY TERRIFIC TIPS

Tips sheets can be a fantastic marketing tool. Assemble a list of helpful tips that are of interest to your target audience, and you can either sell them or use them as bonus items. Your tips could be as few as 10 or as many as 100. A financial advisor could assemble a tips sheet called "Twenty Ways to Save on Tax Planning." A beauty salon could offer "Ten Tips for Ageless Skin." A child-care center could give away "Twenty-five Tips for Child Safety."

Offer your tips as a free bonus for buying a product or registering for your e-zine. Publicity Hound Joan Stewart sends out "89 Reasons to Send a Press Release" to reward newsletter subscribers. If your web site is set up with autoresponders, you can automate the entire delivery process.

Another way to use tips sheets is to offer them to other businesses to give away. When another business uses your tips as a promotional item, you get exposure to potential new clients. By offering something of real value, people will be more likely to hang on to your list and refer to it over and over again, thus providing a consistent reminder of your business. Make sure your contact information and logo are included and that you strike an agreement to include your contact information with anyone who reproduces your tips.

ONLINE CLASSIFIED ADS

A fabulous venue for getting the word out about your business is Craigslist (www.craigslist.org). There is no charge for listing your ad in a variety of categories, and Craigslist has a presence in most major cities. Ads are archived for two weeks, so be sure to resubmit regularly. Try different ads to see what works best. You can even offer a discount or special offer for people who mention the ad when ordering from you.

MAXIMIZE YOUR SIGNATURE

Your e-mail signature is an important billboard for your business and you can make it as long or as detailed as you want to. You can include your contact information, web site URL, and any other details that you want people to know about your company. You can also highlight a product or service, announce a sale, or include your company tagline. Consider modifying your signature periodically to keep the content fresh and interesting.

If you're communicating with the public through e-mail, your signature is essential. You never know where your messages will be forwarded or whose eye you will catch. It's best to avoid inserting images. Many e-mail systems will route your message straight to the trash can if it includes attachments.

Here is an example of the signature that I use:

Stephanie Chandler
Author of *The Business Startup Checklist and Planning Guide: Seize Your Entrepreneurial Dreams!*
http://www.businessinfoguide.com
http://www.bookloverscafe.com
http://www.stephaniechandler.com

P.S. Get info about my new book at
http://www.businessinfoguide.com/book.htm

⚡ HOT TIP ⚡

Make sure you list **http://** in front of your web site URL anytime you post it online. For example: Don't type it like this: www.businessinfoguide.com. Instead type this: http://www .businessinfoguide.com.

While some e-mail providers and web site pages will automatically activate a web site link, many will leave the link static. This means that users will have to copy and paste the link in a browser to view the site. The http://activates your link to make it clickable from most e-mail systems and web pages.

STRATEGIC ALLIANCES

Your business networks can reach to Australia, England, Japan, and back if you want them to. Get in touch with business owners across the Internet and see how you can work together.

The key to successful alliances is to offer up something that is beneficial to both parties. You also want to make sure you are partnering with businesses that reach your target audience. In some cases, you may even want to partner with your competition. You know the old saying, "Keep your friends close and your enemies closer?" When you stop viewing your competition as the enemy, you could uncover some great ways you can complement each other. Here are some ideas:

- ✔ Swap links to each other's web sites.
- ✔ Trade advertising space on web pages.
- ✔ Trade advertising space in e-zines.
- ✔ Publish each other's articles in e-zines.
- ✔ Swap tips sheets or other electronic products for giveaways.
- ✔ Give away each other's tips sheets or eBooks as bonuses with product purchases.
- ✔ Support each other with new product releases. Though your time lines may be different, make sure each is committed to helping with announcements when a new release date approaches.
- ✔ Offer affiliate programs to make it financially worthwhile for others to promote your products. See PayDotCom.com or PayLoadz.com for free affiliate accounts.
- ✔ Coproduce a new product or even a web site. Two small companies that work together can create one big company or even just a campaign. Make sure to put deals like these in writing to keep everyone on the same page.

If your business is small and you want to align with a more established business, you can still create an opportunity to work together. Make sure to personalize your initial contact with the business owner. Send a thoughtful e-mail or pick up the phone and call. Introduce yourself and give a genuine compliment about the business owner's site or product. Suggest ways that you can help him. Then wait and let him offer up some ways to help you. If he has a mailing list of 10,000, and you only have 1,000, offer to run his ad for six months versus the one or three months that he runs yours. If he likes you, he may not even care that you're on different levels of the playing field.

To locate strategic alliance partners, start by searching the Internet for keywords that complement your business. If you run an event-planning business, you could search for hotels, tour companies, catering companies, and travel agents. Notice the sites that are listed in the top 20—those are likely getting the most traffic for your industry.

Once you locate potential partners, start contacting them one by one. You don't have to do this all in one day. In fact, it may be beneficial to start slowly so you can see what kind of response you get to your methods. If your methods aren't working, evaluate and modify your pitch until you see results. Over time you should be able to build up a solid list of key relationships.

As with any business contact, be sure to nurture the relationship. Check in periodically or share an interesting article or piece of news of interest to your strategic partner. Send him kudos when you see his name mentioned in the media or let him know when you've seen his ad somewhere. When you treat business relationships with the same respect you give your friends, you build loyalty that can last a lifetime.

ONLINE GROUPS

If you have a niche product or service, an online group can bring your business some tremendous exposure. Groups are essentially forums on the Internet that allow members to exchange messages about the group's primary subject matter.

When you start a group, you act as the moderator and can make decisions about who can join the group, the types of messages that are allowed, and whether you want members to be able to attach files or information to their posts. You can also send broadcast messages to group members. Visitors to Yahoo's group main site (http://groups.yahoo.com) can search keywords to locate active groups, which can bring a group owner new subscribers with very little effort.

You can start and manage a free group with Yahoo! at http://groups .yahoo.com. Begin by searching some of the existing groups, or by joining one or two to get a feel for how they operate.

Moderating a group can be time consuming so you need to be sure it's worth your effort. However, with enough promotion and word of mouth from new members, membership numbers have the potential to increase rapidly.

FORUMS AND MESSAGE BOARDS

Forums are similar to Yahoo! groups because they encourage participation of visitors. The primary difference is that members do not have to subscribe and there can be numerous subtopics. Some service providers also allow you to run forums right inside your web site.

Denise O'Berry manages an online forum called "Minding Your Own Business" through the Ryze network (http://myob-network.ryze.com). Her forum is targeted toward entrepreneurs and encourages visitors to exchange tips and information. One of the benefits of membership with Ryze is the ability to start your own forum.

Establishing your own forum or message board can attract visitors to your site through keyword searches. Hosting an active forum on your web site can also encourage visitors to return frequently.

Keep in mind the amount of time involved in monitoring message boards as well as the possible legal implications. Angela Hoy, owner of www.writersweekly.com, operates active message boards for writers. One of her boards called "Whispers and Warnings" is a forum that allows writers to log complaints about publishers who didn't pay on time or who do not have ethical business practices.

Hoy was forced to change the way that the message board operates after spending thousands on legal fees to deal with publishers who complained of slander. She also ended up working with law enforcement personnel, including the FBI, in a few circumstances. She provides a great public service, but there was a downside in attempting to allow free speech. The forum still operates, but Hoy personally manages the posts that are allowed and no longer permits the public to freely submit complaints. If you are concerned about the potential content you want to allow on your message board, be sure to seek the counsel of a lawyer before you begin.

FORUM TECHNOLOGY PROVIDERS

- ✔ PHPBB: www.phpbb.com
- ✔ World Crossing: http://wc0.worldcrossing.com
- ✔ BulletinBoards.com: www.bulletinboards.com

GET ACTIVE ON MESSAGE BOARDS

Visiting online forums and message boards may seem like a time waster; however these venues create an opportunity for exposure. When you respond to a message on a popular forum, you can include a signature file with a brief description and a web site URL.

The trick here is to make intelligent posts that readers in your target audience will notice. Not only can this help you build name recognition for yourself and your business, but there is a high likelihood that readers will click-through to check out your web site.

Literally thousands of online forums are available. Start by checking with the trade associations you belong to. Many magazines also have forums. Here is a list of some general business forums:

✔ The community on Ryze offers forums and the chance to network with other members. Free and paid subscriptions are available: www.ryze.com.

✔ LinkedIn offers forums for locating clients, announcing your services, and other business networking opportunities: www.linkedin.com.

✔ Business Owners' Idea Cafe allows entrepreneurs to swap business ideas and advice: www.businessownersideacafe.com/cyberschmooz.

✔ The Small Business Forum offers topics for entrepreneurs: www.small-business-forum.com.

✔ There are more than a dozen topics for small business owners on About.com: www.entrepreneurs.about.com/mpboards.htm. You can also locate forums on other topics at www.about.com.

✔ The forums at Business Know How cover employee issues, business start-up, marketing, and more: www.businessknowhow.com/forum.

✔ If you are a work-at-home mom (WAHM) then check out the forums on the Internet Based Moms site: http://Internetbasedmoms.com/bb.

HOST A FREE DAY

The comic books industry has an annual "Free Comic Book Day" that prompts comic collectors to flock to local comic stores. Select a day to give something away and advertise the heck out of it. Most will not only log on to claim their free prize, but could end up making a purchase from your site as a result.

START AN AFFILIATE PROGRAM

Most of the infopreneurs interviewed for this book offer some kind of affiliate program. An affiliate program is a way to offer incentives to others to help sell your products by paying a commission for each sale. In most cases, you can offer a percentage or flat dollar amount for each sale generated by your affiliates.

The major online shopping cart services provide an option to create your own affiliate program. Some other affiliate services to consider are www.clickbank.com and www.paydotcom.com. Affiliate sales can account for a large percentage of your revenues if marketed correctly.

If you offer affiliate sales, make it as easy as possible for your affiliates to be successful. Offer complete product descriptions and graphic images that they can use on their web sites. You may even consider offering training programs online or with a teleseminar to help your affiliates sell your products.

GET TESTIMONIALS

Whenever anyone says something nice about your business, use it to your advantage. Print testimonials on all marketing materials, in your business location, and on your web site. To obtain testimonials, just ask! Contact your best clients and ask them to write a paragraph about your business. Be sure to get permission to reprint from anyone who provides you with a testimonial.

You can also send testimonials to sites that you admire. Most sites have a place where these are listed and will happily include a reciprocal link back to your site.

HOLD A CONTEST

People love to get stuff for free and contests are a great way to attract new customers. This is also an excellent way to earn exposure for your information products since you can use them as prizes. Be sure to alert the media about your contest. Here are some contest ideas:

- ✔ Have kids color pictures or submit stories related to your business theme.
- ✔ Have customers submit funny business slogans.
- ✔ Hold a poetry contest with a theme related to your business.
- ✔ Have people submit their best solutions to problems related to your business. For example, if you own a garden center, people could submit their best gardening tips. Take this a step further and publish the entries in a booklet when the contest is over.
- ✔ Host a recipe contest if you have a food-related business.

Get creative with your contest ideas. I've seen web site owners host contests as a way of gathering testimonials, and others have given away consulting services as an award for the best story submission. Find something that creates a buzz so you can reel in new traffic and exposure for your products and services.

PREANNOUNCE NEW PRODUCTS

It's never too early to start building excitement around a new product offering. When your product is in the development phase, it is perfectly acceptable to begin mentioning it on your web site and in your e-zine several months before the product will be available. In fact, you can even set up a preorder system to solicit orders prior to the product release. If you do this, make sure you set a safe release date that you know you won't miss.

Infopreneur Profile

Paulette Ensign
San Diego, California
Tips Products International
www.tipsbooklets.com

PUBLICATION:

110 Ideas for Organizing Your Business Life

RETAIL PRICE:

$5.00 single copy—more typically sold in bulk at various prices, or licensed at project rates.

TYPE OF PUBLICATION:

Self-published tips booklet both hard copy and digital formats.

BRIEF DESCRIPTION OF CONTENT:

How-to tips for managing paper, time, space, and interpersonal communication in one's business life.

Who is your target audience for your materials?
Small business owners, corporations, associations, and publications.

Where do you sell your materials?
My web site, direct sales, affiliates and marketing partners.

When did your first publish your material?
1991.

What made you decide to self-publish?
The complete control over production, marketing, and profits.

How does your publication enhance your business?
It has served as a direct marketing tool for my business as well as a new unique revenue stream. It ultimately spurred an entire new business focused on helping individuals and organizations transform their knowledge into tips booklets.

What process did you use to publish?
I modeled my booklet format and writing style after someone's I had seen, and figured out the rest on my own. It was part of a business I already was running. The process was to do a data dump of ideas into a word processing file, refine the contents, have some friends review it, have a graphic designer do the layout, and send it to an offset printing

company to print it. It took several sets of vendors before finding the ones who did the job the way it needed to be done at a price that was workable.

How did your journey to becoming an infopreneur begin?

Way back in 1991, when my organizing business was already eight years old, I spotted an offer for a free copy of a booklet called "117 Ideas for Better Business Presentations."

Well, because I do business presentations, and because the price was right, I sent for it. My first reaction was, "Geez, I could knock something like this out about organizing tips." Then I threw it in a drawer.

Six months later, I was sitting in my office, bored, baffled, and beaten down by the difficulty of selling my consulting services and workshops. I had no money. I mean no money!

I remembered that little booklet. I had no idea how I was going to do it, but something hit me, and I knew I had to produce a booklet on organizing tips.

I started dumping all those ideas I ever had about getting organized onto a file on my computer. I could do one booklet on business organizing tips and another on household organizing tips. Two 16-page tips booklets, each fitting into a number 10 envelope. The first one was "110 Ideas for Organizing Your Business Life" and the second one "111 Ideas for Organizing Your Household."

My first run was 250 copies. That was the most expensive per unit run I made, but I had to get samples to distribute to start making money. It took a few months to pay the printer only $300.

The only way I could think of selling the booklets was by sending a copy to magazines and newspapers, asking them to use excerpts and put an invitation at the bottom for readers to send $3 plus a self-addressed stamped envelope. I had no money to advertise.

Then the orders started dribbling in, envelopes with $3 checks in them or 3 one-dollar bills. This was great stuff. I remember the day the first one arrived. It was like manna from heaven: $3! Of course, the fact that it took about 6 months from first starting to write the booklet until the first $3 arrived somehow didn't matter at that moment.

I cast seeds all over the place, hoping that some would sprout. I found directories of publications at the library and started building my list.

Finally, in February 1992 the big one hit. A 12-page biweekly newsletter with 1.6 million readers ran nine lines of copy about my booklet. They didn't even use excerpts! That sold 5,000 copies of my booklet. I distinctly remember the day I went to my P.O. box and found a little yellow slip in my box. It said, "see clerk."

There was a *tub* of envelopes that had arrived that day, about 250 envelopes as I recall, all with $3 in them.

Round about June, I stopped and assessed what had happened. Was I making any money? By then, I had sold about 15,000 copies of the business and the household organizing tips booklets one copy at a time for $3. When I checked my financial records, I realized I had tediously generated not a ton of money.

And some of the lessons I had learned along the way were expensive ones. I didn't realize my bank was charging me $0.12 for each item deposited until I got my first bank statement with a service charge of $191.

Some very wonderful things happened while selling those 15,000 copies though.

A public seminar company ordered a review copy to consider building another product from my booklet. They did, and I recorded an audio program based on the booklet. I can sell that tape to my clients as well and it led to a 20-minute interview on a major airline's in-flight audio programming during November and December one year.

I was sorting through the envelopes, . . . $3, $3, $1,000, $3, . . . wait a minute. Well, a manufacturer's rep decided to send my booklets to his customers that year instead of an imprinted calendar.

A company asked me to write a booklet that was more specific to their product line.

I got speaking engagements from people who bought the booklet.

One day, a guy I know from a major consumer mail-order catalog company said, "Why don't you license us reprint rights to your booklet. We can buy print cheaper than you, so if you charged us a few cents a unit, you wouldn't have to do production." Well, 18 months later after lots of zigging and zagging, that sale happened: a nonexclusive agreement for them to print 250,000 copies. We exchanged a 10-page contract for a five-digit check.

They provided the booklet free with any purchase in one issue of their catalog and made a 13 percent increase in sales in that issue. They were happy. I was happy.

Midway through that year (August 1994), I discovered CompuServe. My sole purpose for getting online was to market my business. The third day I was online, I saw a forum message from a guy from Italy who had a marketing company there. He told me his client base was small businesses and companies who served small businesses. I told him I had a booklet he might find useful. I sent it to him, he liked it and we struck a deal. He translated, produced, and marketed it, and paid me royalties on all sales. This January he wired several thousand dollars to my checking account from Italy. He made the first sale of 105,000 copies to a magazine that bundled a copy of my booklet with one issue of their publication.

I've also discovered new opportunities for my booklet, and other ways to support the success of my clients:

- Two different companies who produce laminated guides (one hinged, the other spiral bound) licensed my content into their format.
- I write tips booklets for clients by distilling information from their printed material of articles, books, workbooks, e-zines, and interview transcriptions.
- Clients "rent my brain" for an hour at a time or weekly to help them identify and focus their business marketing strategies.
- A fourth language has been added to the formats of my own booklet.
- Almost a million copies of the original organizing booklet have now been sold.

I never could have written a business plan for how this has all unfolded.

How do you market your products?

The primary methods have been (1) publicity excerpts in the editorial pages of magazines; (2) bulk sales directly to corporations, associations, and publications; (3) licensing the rights to reprint the booklet as a booklet; (4) licensing the rights to translate the contents into other languages and formats; (5) electronic publishing and marketing, with digital delivery as well as circulating articles I've written.

I do a fair amount of public speaking both in person and through teleclasses, which also market my materials. Each marketing method has worked to greater and lesser degrees and each has had its limitations. I would not have left out any of them, since each one brought its own successes, some of which I could not have imagined.

What has been the most challenging part of the publishing process?
Pricing.

What has been the most rewarding part of the publishing process?
The endless possibilities of ways to leverage a single booklet manuscript into so many different formats and sales, and the fact I've personally sold over a million copies of my booklet in various languages and formats without spending a penny on advertising or ever going anywhere near a bookstore.

What have you learned from the experience that you would like to share with others?
There is no such thing as a saturated market. Given the billions of quasi-intelligent people there are in just the English-speaking world, there is no way any of us could ever reach everyone who would be our client. It's vital to dissolve any limiting beliefs about what can be done with the contents of a person's publications.

Looking back, is there anything you would do differently?
No, not really. Every step has been an exciting opportunity to explore, learn, and grow.

10

Offline Marketing Techniques: Pounding the Pavement

A goal without a plan is just a wish.
—ANTOINE DE SAINT-EXUPÉRY

Though marketing on the Internet should be an important focus of your overall marketing strategy, there are still many tasks you can accomplish offline to get the word out about your business. Even if your business spans the globe, your local community is accessible and can provide great support for your business.

WRITING EFFECTIVE SALES COPY

Every product you create needs to be supported with powerful sales copy. When you are not personally making the sales pitch, your sales copy is your best chance to reel in a customer. Whether printed on brochures, flyers, or on your web site, writing effective sales copy is essential to product success.

When developing your copy, you want to appeal to your customers *emotions*. Many people buy for emotional reasons and want to know, "What's in it for me?" Here's an example of lackluster sales copy:

Our special report, "101 Career Options," lists a variety of different job options so that you can find a new line of work. Order your copy for $19.95.

Here's a more powerful version of the copy:

If you're tired of reporting in to a job that you don't like and you want to earn more money now, you will find over a hundred ideas for careers that could change your life! Our special report, "101 Money-Making Careers," is loaded with ideas for new job opportunities that you can pursue today. We'll show you how to easily transition into a different field where you will find exciting work and a better quality of life. Don't wait—your new life is waiting for you! Order today for just $19.95.

Notice how the second sales copy example solves a problem—this is far more likely to appeal to a buyer's senses. The copy also contains keywords that trigger a response. There are certain words in the English language that evoke an emotional response. Here are some words and phrases to include in your copy:

Act Now	Entertaining	Now
Amazing	Exclusive	Offer
Approved	Fascinating	Only
Attractive	Genuine	Opportunity
Bargain	Great	Outrageous
Certified	Guaranteed	Outstanding
Colossal	Huge	Phenomenal
Deal	Hurry	Popular
Discount	Immediately	Powerful
Don't Wait	Improve	Practical
Exceptional	Informative	Praised
Extraordinary	Last Chance	Proven
Free	Limited Time	Rare
Get it	Low Cost	Recommended
Gigantic	Lowest Price	Reduced Price
Easy	Massive	Reliable
Endorsed	Money	Remarkable
Enormous	New	Revolutionary

Save	Superior	Unsurpassed
Secrets	Today	Versatile
Sensational	Transform	Wealth
Solution	Tremendous	Wonderful
Special	Unique	
Success	Unparalleled	

Another trick for developing good copy is to ask yourself these questions:

✔ What problem does it solve for your customer?

✔ What benefits would compel someone to purchase this product?

✔ What are the product's key features?

✔ Can you offer a special bonus or create a sense of urgency to purchase this product?

WRITING OP/ED PIECES

The opinion section of any major newspaper can be a great place to get exposure. Study the editorial section and determine what kinds of articles get published there. Send your piece to the editor and include a brief author bio (just one or two sentences with your web site link). You could even contact the editor to suggest your topic and see if he or she would be interested in your article. Although it may be easiest to get your start by writing for your local paper, consider major papers since these reach the largest audiences:

✔ *New York Times:* www.nytimes.com

✔ *San Francisco Chronicle:* http://sfgate.com/chronicle

✔ *Washington Post:* www.washingtonpost.com

✔ *Miami Herald:* www.miami.com/mld/miamiherald

✔ *USA Today:* www.usatoday.com

PUBLIC SPEAKING

You can give educational presentations relating to your subject area at local adult learning centers, colleges, and community centers. Put together an interesting presentation and pitch your topic to local education centers. Many will even pay you to present your topic. Make sure your presentation is informative and not just a pitch for your business. The fact that you engage the audience with helpful advice should be enough to make them want to know more about your business.

Give your presentations through other businesses and venues. All kinds of topics can be offered from tax planning to successful gardening. Contact businesses in your area and offer to give your presentation to their customers for free. The following businesses like to host these events:

- ✔ Bookstores
- ✔ Medical offices
- ✔ Financial centers
- ✔ Real estate offices
- ✔ Coffee shops
- ✔ Hardware stores
- ✔ Restaurants

WRITTEN CORRESPONDENCE

The influx of e-mail usage has nearly done away with personal letters and communication. A personal note is a wonderful way to stand out against the pack and create a lasting impression. Take a moment to craft a note or letter for any of the following reasons:

- ✔ To thank a customer for their business
- ✔ To welcome a new client
- ✔ To thank a business associate
- ✔ To apologize for an error
- ✔ To recognize a birthday or anniversary
- ✔ To thank someone for a referral
- ✔ To offer kudos for something done well

Notes can be handwritten on generic thank-you cards or you can order some special business stationery for this purpose. I keep note cards and postcards handy either to mail alone or to insert in a package or product shipment.

RECOGNIZING HOLIDAYS

Offbeat holidays and special event weeks are abundant. Events from "Take Your Pet to Work Day" and "National Small Business Month" to "Secretaries Day" and "Home Office Day" are nationally recognized and listed in *Chase's Calendar of Events,* published by McGraw Hill. Pick up a copy of the book to get ideas for promotion opportunities, or create your own special event by submitting it to Chase's for consideration: http://books.mcgraw-hill.com/getpage .php?page=chases_intro.php&template=chases.

Be sure to capitalize on traditional holidays by finding a unique angle to attract media attention to your business. If you have a crafts business, Christmas and Hanukkah can be excellent times to develop special promotions.

PROMOTIONS, CONTESTS, GIVEAWAYS, AND CHARITY EVENTS

Brainstorm ideas for a contest with clearly defined rules and an attractive reward. Pay attention to how other businesses are running these promotions. Many restaurants have a jar to drop in your business card for a weekly drawing to receive a free lunch. This is an excellent way to build up a newsletter database since you will gather cards with e-mail and mailing addresses. You could also hold a coloring contest for kids—let the local schools know and offer awards to the top entries.

One Northern California restaurant announced a "Bald Tuesday" promotion, where balding individuals eat free on Tuesdays. Sound ridiculous? The media loved it. The restaurant was featured on local news programs and eventually received national attention.

You can also use this strategy to partner with other businesses. If you own a restaurant, you could have your local Holiday Inn give dinner gift certificates for $10 to hotel guests during check-in. If you own a car wash, you could have the local car dealerships give a certificate for a free wash with all car purchases.

Examine what other businesses in your area are offering their customers to get ideas. I've held special promotions at my bookstore where kids get to pick out a book for free. Use your imagination and create something fun that the public will respond to. Don't forget to send a press release announcing the promotion.

You can also offer your products, services, or gift certificates for charity auctions and events. This will get you exposure to everyone who attends the event and build loyalty with members of the organization you are supporting—not to mention a potential tax write-off!

DISTRIBUTING FLYERS

You can use templates to design your own brochures and flyers. Microsoft Publisher provides an impressive array of free templates. You can also download templates from Microsoft: http://office.microsoft.com/en-us/templates/default.aspx.

Depending on the size and scope of your business, you can distribute flyers door to door in your neighborhood or hire some kids to do it for you. Flyers can also be left on the windshields of cars in busy parking lots.

A local Realtor canvassed my neighborhood just before Memorial Day. She stuck an inexpensive American flag in the lawn in front of every house and then left her business card on each doorstep. This was an impressive way to get the attention of an entire neighborhood. The effort left us feeling a bit more patriotic as we drove through the neighborhood and admired all the flags waving in the wind. If this Realtor wanted to continue maximizing the impact, she could do it again for Independence Day, Veteran's Day, and all the other patriotic holidays and brand herself as "the flag lady."

Many local businesses will allow you to display your cards and brochures. Potential venues include:

- ✔ Car washes
- ✔ Bookstores
- ✔ Coffee shops
- ✔ Apartment buildings (near mailboxes or in laundry rooms)
- ✔ Churches
- ✔ Student centers

✔ Community centers
✔ Retirement centers
✔ Fitness centers
✔ Subways and bus depots
✔ Fraternities and sororities
✔ Libraries

MAKING YOUR BUSINESS CARD A KEEPER

Give people a reason to keep your card and refer to it again and again. You can have the back side of your card printed with some useful information. For example, you could include a yearly calendar, tips related to your business, or a handy chart.

At the bookstore, we have a rubber stamp that we use to stamp the back of business cards and transform them into inexpensive coupons. The stamp says the following:

Customer Rewards Card
Bring this card back to save 10 percent off your next purchase!
Expires: _____

We handwrite in an expiration date, typically the last day of the following month, and drop one of these cards in the bag with every purchase. This gives customers an incentive to return in a short time and has been a very popular program.

DIRECT MAIL

Create a newsletter or special brochure to mail to your prospects. Compile or purchase a mailing list that reaches your target audience. Send repeat mailings with new and interesting information to maximize exposure and find out which tactics work best. Visit the U.S. Post Office (www.usps.gov) for details on receiving bulk mail rates.

YELLOW PAGES

Ads in the phone book are expensive but crucial for many kinds of businesses. Internet companies are the exception since to advertise in the yellow pages across the world would cost more than even Donald Trump could afford. If you want to be listed in the yellow pages, be sure to get your ad in early since the phone book only comes out once each year and you don't want to miss the deadline. You may also have to place ads in several books, since most areas have more than one company that distributes phone books.

When deciding on your advertising strategy, evaluate the ads that comparable businesses are running. How can you compete with them? Just because an ad is bigger does not mean it is the most effective. Study ads throughout the phone book and decide which ones you like best.

Take your time when working with your yellow pages ad representative to identify the best package offering for your business. The phone company releases new packages and programs each year, and it is not easy to sift through all the offerings (which they probably won't send you in print form, so you will have to rely on a salesperson to explain your options). Take notes when talking to your sales representative and ask her to show you examples of what your money can buy.

Discuss advertising in multiple cities if it makes sense for your business. If you're in a small town, you may want to run ads in neighboring cities or in the phone book for the nearest big city. Most yellow pages companies offer discounts for multiple listings.

ADS IN LOCAL MAGAZINES AND NEWSPAPERS

This is one of the more expensive venues for promotion and only works well for certain types of businesses. Beware of offers that are less expensive because the ad placement is not ideal. Consider what publications and where in the publication your business should be seen. Advertising contacts are easily located in the publication's masthead or on their web site. The smaller neighborhood newspapers are going to be far less expensive than city newspapers.

STARTING A REFERRAL PROGRAM

Offer your customers some incentive to refer business to you. You could give them something for free (a discount, gift certificate, or product) for sending people your way. One beauty salon mails a $5 gift certificate to everyone who refers a friend. Consider offering something similar since word-of-mouth referrals can bring in some of your best clientele.

GETTING CREATIVE WITH GIFT CERTIFICATES

Gift certificates are great for business because they cost you next to nothing; they bring in cash; and often they are either not redeemed or the redeemer spends more than the certificate's worth.

Get your customers to buy gift certificates by offering them a special bonus. For example: *Buy a gift certificate for $20 or more and receive $5 off your next purchase with us.* When customers purchase a gift certificate, you then give them an extra certificate worth $5 and dated for use the following month only. This means that these customers must return to you the following month and, if they do, will probably spend more than the $5 you've given them.

BUSINESS NETWORKING

Networking isn't just for realtors, it's a valuable tool for any savvy business owner. Meeting people in a variety of industries can lead to all kinds of opportunities. I didn't understand the value of networking until I stopped to realize how it has enhanced my business. Think about the people you know. How have your relationships led to other opportunities?

There is an art to business networking and creating alliances. For some people, the idea of striking up a conversation with strangers is terrifying. For a lucky few, it comes naturally. But the advantages of building your business networks can far outweigh the struggle.

We often hear about the importance of networking, yet we rarely hear about *why* it is so important. No matter what kind of business you have, whether you're an independent contractor, store owner, infopreneur, professional speaker, or doctor, business networks can open up new opportunities for your business.

ADVANTAGES OF NETWORKING

✔ **Opportunity to meet potential clients:** No matter where you go, you have the chance to meet people who could potentially become clients for your business.

✔ **Locate business partners:** As you get to know someone new, you may find that you have common interests or goals. If so, find a way to work together.

✔ **Increased word of mouth:** Some of the best kind of advertising that money cannot buy is word of mouth. The more people who learn about you and your products, the more chance you have to spread the word about your offerings.

✔ **Develop six degrees of separation:** You never know where a new alliance can lead. I've had friendly business contacts refer me to speaking engagements (which then led to other speaking engagements), media exposure (which led to a slew of new clients), new business opportunities (that generated exposure and income), and marketing campaigns (spreading my reach with little cost or effort). Your new client could introduce you to another associate, and that person could introduce you to yet another person, and so on.

✔ **Learn something new:** Savvy business leaders know that to stay at the top of their game, they need to continually learn more about their industry. You have the opportunity to learn something from each person you meet.

✔ **Challenge yourself:** When you meet someone whose level of success is higher than your own, challenge yourself to take your business to the next level. Let that person's success inspire you to do more.

TWENTY-EIGHT STEPS TO SUCCESSFUL NETWORKING

1. **Evaluate your handshake.** This may seem like a no-brainer, but a lot of people drop the ball on this one. Your handshake should be firm and confident without breaking bones. This is true for both women and men.

2. Watch your body language. Nothing is more subtle than body language. Watch a roomful of people to see how each person looks different. Confident people stand up tall, hold their heads high, and often talk with their hands. People who are shy or uncomfortable cross their arms in front of them, hang their head low, and look disinterested. Who would you rather approach? Someone who looks miserable and closed off or someone who is confident and relaxed? Watch yourself in a mirror. See how different you look when your posture is strong and your arms are at your side.

3. Carry multiple business cards. If you have more than one business, you should have cards for each business. Always be prepared and carry sets of each of your cards to all events.

4. Maximize the value of your business card. Make sure the information on your card is up to date and accurate. There is nothing worse than someone who hands you a card and says, "Oh, but my phone number has changed. Let me write it in there for you." Even if you have new cards on order, you can purchase blank card stock at the office supply store and print some temporary cards so you always reflect a professional image.

5. Prepare an elevator pitch. You should have a 30-second sound byte that you can give whenever you meet someone new. Your pitch should explain who you are and what you do and should be succinct and compelling. Start by writing it down and practice your delivery.

6. Define your purpose. Attending networking events won't have much value if you don't know why you are there. Are you interested in finding clients? Locating new business partners? Define your goals so you can make the most of your efforts.

7. Say cheese. Smiling at someone instantly puts the person at ease, and it is human nature to mirror the other person. Notice how when you smile at someone, the person automatically smiles back. The added benefit is that smiling has a magical power to cause a person to feel better. If someone is having a bad day and you smile and make her smile, you have subconsciously given her a reason to like you.

8. Crack 'em up. Humor is a wonderful icebreaker. Avoid inappropriate jokes or comments, but try to inject some humor into your conversations. People who are funny are naturally magnetic to others. You can still be a serious businessperson with a good sense of humor.

9. Use small talk. When meeting or introducing yourself to a new contact, start with small talk. Ask the contact what he does, where he lives, how far he traveled to get to the event, or what brought him to the event.

Develop a standard list of questions you will use to start and maintain small talk with new people.

10. Keep moving. Don't hold up the wall or stay in one place for too long. Make the most of your networking time by moving often and ending conversations that have reached their maximum value. If you want to move on from the person you are talking to, you could say, "It's been a pleasure talking with you. I have some other people I need to meet so I hope we can keep in touch."

11. Offer your business card. The best time to exchange business cards is typically near the end of your conversation. Handing the contact your card will usually prompt her to give you hers in exchange. If this doesn't happen automatically, simply ask.

12. Work a table. If you are seated at a table with new contacts, introduce yourself and ask the others to do the same. You can act as the host of the table by instigating conversation. Ask each person why he is there, what he does, what he hopes to get from the event, and so on.

13. Remember to offer value. Networking should be a two-way street. If you want people to help you, you should offer something that helps them. Offer up interesting contacts or resources and keep the relationship reciprocal.

14. Never monopolize a conversation. There is nothing more unappealing than someone who does nothing but talk about herself. Make sure your interactions always go two ways.

15. Ask questions. People love to talk about themselves. Ask questions that evoke more than a Yes or No answer. By asking questions and showing genuine interest in the answers, you automatically build a rapport with the people you are talking to. They will most likely leave the conversation remembering that they liked you.

16. Know when to zip your lip. You might be surprised by how much you can learn about someone when you get quiet. A pause in conversation can lead the other person to grasp for something to say—you never know what you might learn.

17. Drop a line. You can send an e-mail or better yet, a handwritten note, to let the person know that you enjoyed meeting him. Try to point out something specific that you talked about to jog the person's memory in case he met a lot of people and can't remember exactly who you are. For example, you could say, "It was a pleasure meeting you at the cocktail reception. I enjoyed our conversation about Minnesota. I hope we can keep in touch and find a way to work together in the future."

18. Follow through. If you offered to send something, like an article or referral, make sure to follow through on your promises. Send any materials within a week of meeting.

19. Organize your contacts. New people you meet may not fill an immediate need in your networking strategy, but could be a good resource down the line. File the names of every person you meet in a contacts database with a note about when and where you met and what your conversation was about.

20. Remember details. I once had a dentist that I actually enjoyed seeing because I always found it remarkable that he remembered details about me even if I hadn't seen him in two years. He would say, "How is your job going? The last time I saw you, you had just gotten promoted." I eventually realized that he made notes in my file after each visit, but even knowing this, I still appreciated that he personalized our interactions. You will meet a lot of people in your business life and aren't likely to remember all the details. Be sure to make notes in your contacts database even if the items seem trivial. For example, for Joe Schmoe you could note: "Going to Hawaii in December, has two teenage daughters, Raider fan, likes vodka tonics." Check his card prior to your next meeting so you have a few conversation starters ready.

21. Refer your contacts. If someone mentions he is building a web site, offer up the contact information for a great web site designer that you know. If someone mentions that she is going on vacation, recommend your pet sitter. No matter how insignificant this may seem, it can earn you loyalty with both those you refer and the people you refer them to. Eventually this good karma will come back around.

22. Let them know. If you see one of your contacts mentioned in the media or notice a new glossy ad in a trade magazine, drop an e-mail and let the person know. You could say, "Hey, I saw the article about you in *Business Today*. Congratulations!"

23. Offer an invitation to lunch or coffee. Though we all have busy schedules, we also have to take time to eat. If you want to spend some extended time with your new contact, offer to buy lunch or coffee. Most people appreciate a free meal and a chance to interact with someone wh is engaging.

24. Keep it light. If you make plans to meet a business contact for a meal, avoid launching right into a business discussion. It's best to keep the conversation light and informal at least until the food arrives. Start by developing a rapport and talking about personal topics (not too personal!) and then work your way into a business discussion.

25. Hold a networking event. If you want to increase your business contacts on your own terms, host your own networking event. Invite local trade organizations, peers, clients, and business associates. Offer basic refreshments like coffee and inexpensive cookies or step it up a notch and cater in some food. Encourage people to mingle and trade business cards. This can be a wonderful way to showcase your business.

26. Join the Chamber of Commerce. Networking opportunities abound and you can make some great connections by getting in touch with your local business community. Make sure to attend events and participate in all chamber-sponsored programs.

27. Join local trade organizations. Many organizations hold regular meetings and free seminars, providing you with another opportunity to make valuable contacts.

28. Join everything. Even the PTA (Parent/Teacher's Association) can be a great place to network. Join book clubs, writers' groups, or any groups of interest to you, even if they don't directly relate to your business. Get known by everyone. They will associate you with your business as soon as they get to know you; your mere presence at functions could serve as a reminder and cause members to want to do business with you. Before long you will have an excellent database of contacts and will begin to develop a web of opportunities.

Infopreneur Profile

Michelle Dunn
Never Dunn Publishing LLC
Plymouth, New Hampshire
www.michelledunn.com and www.credit-and-collections.com

PUBLICATIONS:

- *Become the Squeaky Wheel: A Credit & Collections Guide for Everyone* (trade paperback, $29.99)
- *Starting a Collection Agency: How to Make Money Collecting Money* (eBook, $29.99; trade paperback, $33.99)

- *Effective Collection Agency Forms and Letters* (eBook, $19.95)
- *How to Help You Get Paid: Credit and Collection Forms and Letters* (eBook, $9.95; trade paperback $12.95)
- *How to Get Your Customers to Pay: Fast, Easy, Effective Letters* (eBook, $19.95)

Who is your target audience for your materials?

Small & large business owners, collection attorneys, and agency owners.

Where do you sell your materials?

My own web site, collection software web sites, debt collection web sites, Amazon, Barnes & Noble, Borders, Waldenbooks, and small bookstores.

What made you decide to self-publish?

I usually do everything I can myself to so I can learn about it and be more successful. I never even considered not self-publishing.

How does your publication enhance your business?

It enhanced my business so much that I sold my business to write and publish full time. I had started M.A.D. Collection Agency and ran it very successfully for eight years and sold it December 2004.

What was the process you used to publish?

I read books, started a publishing company, and networked online and off.

How do you market your materials? What marketing strategies have and haven't worked?

Online with a web site and exchanging links. I used my network of contacts from my 18 years of doing debt collection to exchange links, write articles, and network. I use direct mail and go to bookstores and ask them to carry my books and promotional materials. I went to the Book Expo of America in New York and met a lot of people to network with. I also manage a credit and collections community with over 600 members and network through that and my newsletter, the Collection Connection.

What has been the most challenging part of the publishing process?

Selling the books once I have them!

What has been the most rewarding part of the publishing process?

People calling and writing that my books helped them so much! That is so great!

What have you learned from the experience that you would like to share with others?

I really like self-publishing because you get total control and total money when you sell a book. Learn how to market before you publish your books!

Looking back, is there anything you would do differently?

More premarketing before the book is published.

11

Catch a Buzz: Book Marketing

Outside of a dog, a book is man's best friend. Inside of a dog, it's too dark to read.

—GROUCHO MARX

Simply publishing a book does not guarantee that it will sell. In fact, there is a greater likelihood that your books will collect dust on a shelf unless you are working hard at marketing them.

In a survey called "The Business Impact of Writing a Book" issued by RainToday.com, the authors surveyed indicated their top marketing tactics (the 16 tactics are listed here in order of popularity):

1. Internet marketing
2. Trade magazine coverage
3. Marketed to existing clients
4. Newspaper coverage
5. Marketed by association
6. Marketed to own newsletter list
7. Third-party newsletter coverage
8. Directly to companies

9. Radio coverage
10. Marketed through catalogs
11. Marketed directly to bookstores
12. Marketed to colleges/graduate schools
13. Trade show marketing
14. TV coverage
15. Book-signing events
16. Marketed to libraries

Following is a three-part plan for marketing your book. By implementing as many of these strategies as your time allows, you should be well on your way to publishing success.

STAGE ONE: BEFORE YOUR BOOK IS PUBLISHED

So you're writing a book—congratulations! The simple fact that you are an author will open doors you never expected to walk through and help you establish authority in your field. But before you finish writing that manuscript, you should develop a master plan for your promotion efforts.

GET ORGANIZED

The very first step in this process is to start a marketing journal. A basic spiral notebook will do. Use it to keep a list of your marketing ideas and keep it with you at all times. You should be generating ideas constantly and this will help you keep track and prioritize them.

You may also want to keep a file folder handy so you can fill it with clippings from magazines and mailers. Whenever you come across something interesting in the mail or you read an interesting article in a magazine, clip it out and stick it in your folder. You will be glad you did.

ESTABLISH A WEB SITE

Every author should have a writer's web site. Even if you already manage a web site for your business, a separate author site can be useful for dealing with the public (your fans!), contacting editors and publishers, and promoting your work. The following are some author web sites to give you some ideas:

✔ www.kickstartguy.com

✔ www.twowriters.net

✔ www.barbarawinter.com

✔ www.stephaniechandler.com (my site)

Your writer's site should act as an online press kit by providing the information the media needs to cover your story. Make sure your site includes the following information:

✔ Author's bio with any credentials listed

✔ Author's contact information

✔ Publicist contact information (if applicable)

✔ Clips of articles you have published

✔ Clips of articles published about you

✔ Lists of memberships and affiliations

✔ An overview of your book

✔ Details about the publisher including contact information

✔ A way to order the book (a link to your publisher or Amazon.com will work)

✔ Book reviews

✔ Testimonials

✔ Archived press releases

✔ Schedule of events/author appearances

✔ Excerpts from your book(s)

✔ Articles written by you or others

Be sure to set up a way to preorder your book. You can begin accepting orders as early as two months ahead of the release date. If you don't use an online shopping cart service, you can create a simple shopping cart button with Paypal (www.paypal.com).

American Author is a company that specializes in web sites for authors and offers a slick tool for creating and managing one. Visit www.americanauthor

.com for details. Also see Chapter 8 for more information on how to design and host a web site.

JOIN WRITERS' GROUPS

If you aren't already a member of any writers' groups, you may want to consider joining or attending some meetings to find one that is a good fit for you. Writers' groups come in all shapes and sizes. Some meet weekly, bi-monthly, or monthly. Some have guest speakers—people who are experts in their field (authors, agents, and other publishing professionals). Some function as critique groups—allowing members to share their work and get valuable feedback.

Writers' groups are a great place to network and expand your knowledge. Most groups consist of a mix of published and aspiring writers. Some may write books, while others may write for newspapers and magazines. Each group has different dynamics and goals, so you may have to attend different meetings until you find a group that is right for you.

To locate writers' groups in your area, try the following:

✔ Check with your local library and bookstore to see if any groups are available there.

✔ Search the Internet for your city. For example, if you live in Dallas, you could search the Internet with keyword combinations: "Dallas Writers," "Writers' Group Dallas," or "Dallas Writing."

✔ Visit www.craigslist.org. Most major cities have a presence on this free site. Visit the "Community" category where you will find links to activities, groups, and events. Search for writers' group announcements, or post your own message and let visitors know you are seeking a group.

✔ Read the community calendar in your local newspapers. These groups often post their meeting times in local calendars to encourage attendance.

ONLINE NEWSLETTERS AND WRITERS' RESOURCES

In addition to trade associations and writers' groups, a wealth of information for writers is available online. Many sites offer articles, market listings, book promotion information, and newsletters. The following are some of the best sites to find writing resources:

- ✔ **Writers Weekly** offers resources for magazine markets and self-published books: www.writersweekly.com.
- ✔ **Writers Net** is for writers, editors, agents, and publishers and includes discussion forums: www.writers.net.
- ✔ **Media Bistro** targets anyone who deals with content—writers, publishers, editors, and so on—and offers forums, media events, and other writing-related resources: www.mediabistro.com.
- ✔ **Absolute Write** offers freelance markets and information for authors: www.absolutewrite.com.
- ✔ **Publisher's Marketplace** provides publishing industry news and resources for publishers, editors, and agents: www.publishersmarketplace.com.
- ✔ **Para Publishing** is Dan Poynter's site for self-publishers. His weekly newsletter is loaded with tips and information: www.parapublishing.com.
- ✔ **The Book Promotion Newsletter is published by Francine Silverman.** There is a nominal subscription fee and the content includes interesting tips and shared resources for book marketing: www.bookpromotionnewsletter.com.

If you are interested in freelance writing (getting paid to write for magazines), the following resources will be helpful:

- ✔ **Writers Market** is a subscription-based service from the folks at *Writer's Digest* that allows you to search for market information for consumer and trade magazines, newspapers, and literary agents: www.writersmarket.com.
- ✔ **Funds for Writers** details paying freelance writing markets and weekly newsletter: www.fundsforwriters.com.
- ✔ **Freelance Success** is a subscription-based service with online forums for sharing market info and advice. Writers on this forum command $1+ per word and write for the big national publications: www.freelancesuccess.com.

Subscribe to Writers' Magazines

If you want to become a serious writer, you can learn a lot by reading industry magazines. The following are the most popular print magazines:

- ✔ *Writers Digest:* www.writersdigest.com
- ✔ *The Writer:* www.writermag.com
- ✔ *Poets & Writers Magazine:* www.pw.org
- ✔ *Publisher's Weekly* is a publishing industry standard for learning about trends in the marketplace: www.publishersweekly.com. Because the subscription price is hefty, you may want to read this one at your local library. There is no charge to subscribe to their e-zine.

Utilize Your Business

If you run a business in a field related to your book, maximize the opportunity to promote your book with your customers and business associates. You can provide details about your book on your web site, in newsletters to customers, and even at your physical place of business. Look for ways to use your business to sell your book and start generating some buzz early on.

Assemble an Overview

You will want to have an overview of your book handy for several reasons. You can use it as part of your press kit for the media, for obtaining quotes and testimonials, and other promotion opportunities. If you have a web site, put your overview on a hidden page and send the link out as needed. Your overview should be persuasive and should convince a reader that your book is fantastic.

The following is a list of content to include in your overview:

- ✔ A good description of the book—similar to your book jacket copy
- ✔ Table of contents
- ✔ At least two sample chapters
- ✔ Any relevant testimonials
- ✔ A brief author's bio

OBTAIN TESTIMONIALS

One of the most overlooked areas of promotion is testimonials from influential celebrities. Many first-time authors think these are impossible to get. The good news is that they're not impossible at all—it just takes a little bit of work.

Even more good news is that many authors don't have time to read your entire manuscript and will give you a testimonial based on a few sample chapters and information you provide in your book overview. While you should offer to send your entire manuscript, start by sending your overview and a sample chapter and see if that's enough.

The first step is to make a list of people you would like to get testimonials from. Consider your favorite authors who write in a similar genre. Better yet, look for books in your field with well-known authors and add them to your list. Even some of the biggest authors out there may be willing to help you out if you can impress them enough.

You will want to write to each author personally with your request. Make your letter professional yet inject some of your personality into it. It will help tremendously if you are familiar with the author's work and can mention this in your letter. Most authors should have a web site where you can locate a postal mail or e-mail address.

The following is a copy of the e-mail that I sent to Barbara Winter, a well-known author and speaker. And this letter worked; she wrote back within a day and agreed to provide me with a quote:

Hi Barbara,

I read *Making a Living Without a Job* several years ago and enjoyed it so much that I bought copies for two friends—great job! I was in the Silicon Valley for 11 years before I gave it all up to open a bookstore in Sacramento and focus on my writing goals—and it was the best decision I've ever made!

I'm writing to you because I'm at a crossroads. I've finished my first book and now face the daunting challenge of begging for testimonials. So with that said, do you think you would consider writing just a few short sentences for my book? Here's the scoop:

The title is *The Business Startup Checklist and Planning Guide: Seize Your Entrepreneurial Dreams!* It will be published in Aug/Sept by Aventine press. I also run a web site for entrepreneurs and my goal is to help others achieve their dreams, just as I have. Corporate America gave me an ulcer before my thirtieth birthday—it just wasn't worth it!

If you would be at all interested in helping to support the dreams of a first-time writer who has a lot to say and more books to follow, I would forever be grateful. An overview and sample chapters are available on my web site at: http://www.businessinfoguide.com/bookoverview.htm.

Thanks for your time—and best of luck with your thriving career.

Best regards,
Stephanie Chandler

STAGE TWO: WHILE YOUR BOOK IS BEING PUBLISHED

You could drive yourself crazy if you simply sat around waiting for your book to come off the press, and it wouldn't be a very good business decision either. Once your manuscript is complete, the real work is only just beginning.

UPDATE YOUR E-MAIL SIGNATURE

Your e-mail signature is a powerful tool that you should take full advantage of. E-mail signatures can be as long or as short as you like. Before your book is even available, let the world know by adding it to your e-mail signature. After your name, list the title of your book along with a link to more details. Be sure to use this signature on any online posts as well.

START ASSEMBLING A MEDIA LIST

One of your priorities should be to get media attention for your book. It is the most inexpensive form of promotion, as well as one of the most powerful. When the media hypes a book, people listen and may be more inclined to accept the recommendation than if it came from a friend.

You will use your media list to send press releases and pitch story ideas. Your ultimate goal should be to reach a national audience, though you should start locally. Your local media outlets should be interested in your book simply because of your geographic proximity. Every community loves local celebrities, and now is your chance to become one where you live.

To build your media contact list, visit the web sites of all the local news stations, radio stations, newspapers, and magazines. You will want to contact editors and show producers who will be interested in your topic. If you have a business book, contact the business editor. If you have a cookbook, contact the features editor or lifestyles editor.

Use a spreadsheet or contact management system such as Microsoft Outlook to track your list of contacts. Add each person's name, title, e-mail address, and phone number. In addition to the media outlets in your immediate area, spread out your list to those in large surrounding cities. If you come from a different area, also locate the media outlets there so you can tailor your pitch as a native of XYZ town.

Create a separate list for national media contacts. Consider all the major media outlets where you think your story would be of interest. Visit each web site to gather the same information as you did for your local list.

Solicit Printing of Excerpts

Once you have begun compiling your media list, you can solicit print publications and offer them excerpts of your book for reprint. When you offer to print an excerpt of a book in a newspaper or magazine before the book is in print, you are offering first serial rights. Note: If you are publishing with a traditional publisher, make sure you have the right to solicit reprints.

Select 6 or 12 topics from your book that could be reprinted as excerpts. You can always tweak them to fit the publication style or length requirements. Contact newspaper and magazine editors who might be interested in your excerpts and offer them for reprint. You may want to send an individual sample of an excerpt, or send a list of available topics and let them choose.

Don't waste your time writing to the editor of *Woman's Day* to pitch an article about men's health. Make sure your concept fits the needs of the publication so you don't waste your time or theirs. Since magazines usually round up all their articles several months in advance, you should contact them early to try to have the article printed around your book release date.

Trade magazines and the smaller magazines that you don't find near the checkout counter at the grocery store are probably going to be more receptive to publishing an excerpt from a new author. This process takes time and patience and you may have to query 30 publications until you find one that sticks. Be persistent.

Here is a sample based on a letter I used for my book:

Dear Ms. Smith,

My new book, *The Business Startup Checklist and Planning Guide: Seize Your Entrepreneurial Dreams!* will be out this fall. Would you be interested in running an excerpt from the book?

I have a number of topics to choose from including:

- Start an eBay Trading Assistant Business
- Tips for Buying an Existing Business
- Venues for Launching a Product Business
- How to Create an Operations Manual
- How to Create an Employee Manual
- The Business Startup Checklist
- Ten Easy Businesses to Start

I would be happy to send you any of these articles for consideration. I hope you will agree that these topics would be a great fit for your readers.

I am the owner of Book Lovers Bookstore in Sacramento, California, and BusinessInfoGuide.com, a directory of resources for entrepreneurs. I am also a published freelance writer, and sample clips can be found at www.stephaniechandler.com/bio.

More information about the book is available at www.businessinfoguide .com/book. Jay Conrad Levinson calls it "mandatory reading for entrepreurs!"

I appreciate your time and consideration, and hope to hear from you soon.

Best regards,
Stephanie Chandler

SOLICIT BOOK REVIEWS

Now is a good time to solicit book reviews, media attention, book buyers, and bookstore attention. The simplest way to do this is to create a flyer that outlines the details of your book and estimated publication date. You can either include a tear-off coupon at the bottom of the flyer or insert a postage-paid postcard that the letter recipient can send back to request a complimentary review copy of your book. Send your letter to the following sources:

- ✔ Bookstore owners/buyers
- ✔ Trade associations
- ✔ Specialty stores
- ✔ Catalog companies (visit www.businessinfoguide.com/catalogs.htm for a list of catalog directories)
- ✔ Local media (newspaper editors or columnists, TV show producers, radio show producers)

Some influential publications will only write book reviews from galley copies. A galley is an early copy of a manuscript, often printed without complete editing and with a cover that simply has text with the title, author, publisher details, and estimated release date.

Many print shops can publish galley copies for you if your publisher can't. They will be more costly than your regular book since you only need a dozen or so copies, but they can be worth it if you can garner reviews from big publications. Galleys should be sent out four to six months prior to publication. Some of the large newspapers will also accept galleys for review. Check the web site of each publication for submission guidelines. In most cases, you should include a press release or a data sheet about the book.

The following are influential industry magazines that accept galley copies:

- ✔ *Publisher's Weekly:* www.publishersweekly.com
- ✔ *Library Journal:* www.libraryjournal.com
- ✔ *Kirkus Reviews:* www.kirkusreviews.com
- ✔ *ForeWord Magazine:* www.forewordmagazine.com

Amazon.com employs category editors who may review your book and assist with promotion. They will not guarantee a review or even notify you of receipt of the book, but it's worth the price of postage to submit your book along with any promotional materials to:

Editorial Department
Category Editor (e.g., Travel Editor)
Amazon.com
705 Fifth Ave South, 5th floor
Seattle, WA 98104

There is very little you can do to follow up with the Amazon editor, other than to wait and check your book's details page for updates.

⚡ HOT TIP ⚡

To locate reviewers of books in your genre, sign up for Google's Alert service (www.google.com). You can indicate keywords and Google will send you an e-mail when those keywords show up in the news or across the Internet. This is a great way to stay on top of your industry. I keep an alert for "business book review" so I can monitor book reviews and compile an ongoing list of reviewers and publications that review business books. Give it a try—it's free!

START GENERATING BUZZ

There are literally hundreds of ways you can think outside the box and generate buzz and opportunities for your book. Use some of the following suggestions and develop some creative strategies of your own. Think about people you know, the networks you belong to, and ways that you can get people excited about your book.

CONTACT BLOGGERS

Blogs are spreading like wildfire across the Internet and many bloggers have loyal and dedicated audiences for their daily messages. Contact bloggers who discuss topics related to your book and ask if they would be interested in a review copy. A blogger with a big audience could bring you even more book sales than a standard book review. Many bloggers are signed up with Amazon.com's affiliate program and will happily promote your book along with a link so they can get a small piece of the pie.

And if you find these blogs fascinating, why not start your own? To locate blogs and blog services, check out these sites:

✔ www.globeofblogs.com
✔ www.blogger.com
✔ www.blogsforsmallbusiness.com
✔ www.typepad.com
✔ www.blogcritics.com

CONTACT ALL SOURCES REFERENCED IN BOOK

If your book mentions any companies, business owners, authors, or web sites—and it probably does—get in touch with those mentioned. Let them know you have given them some free PR in your book. You could ask if they would be interested in reselling the book or offering a link to it from their web site. Think strategically. How could your book benefit that business? Make your pitch.

UPDATE BIO ON ALL MEMBERSHIP DIRECTORIES

This is an easy task to overlook. Take an inventory of all the organizations and web sites where you have a profile listed and visit all of them. Update your profile to indicate that you are the author of XYZ book. Don't forget sites like Yahoo! and Amazon.com—anywhere that you have updated personal information that is publicly available.

PRINT BOOKMARKS, POSTCARDS, BUSINESS CARDS, AND BROCHURES

Your printed materials can be invaluable promotional tools. Make sure you have a quality image of your book cover and use it on all your correspondence. Bookmarks can be handed out at every event and left in bookstores. Postcards and brochures can be mailed out to customers, media, bookstores, businesses, and everyone you can think of. You should give business cards to everyone you encounter. You can even stuff any of these items into remittance envelopes when you pay your bills.

Microsoft Publisher is an excellent tool for designing these materials yourself, but you can also elect to hire a graphic designer if your budget allows. Send a request for quote (RFQ) to all local print shops to compare pricing. Printing locally will save money on shipping, though you may also want to check the prices of some of the online companies:

- ✔ www.vistaprint.com
- ✔ www.iprint.com
- ✔ www.gotprint.com

E-Mail Campaigns

A popular method for generating book sales is to implement an e-mail marketing campaign. Aside from your own mailing list, you should contact your peers and ask them to participate. Some authors have had such tremendous success with these marketing efforts that they have seen their books skyrocket to the top of Amazon.com's best seller list.

Here are eight steps to follow to make this strategy work for you:

1. Make a list of the people you know and even those that you don't who have significant mailing list databases. Anyone who works in your general industry and reaches your target audience can participate in a campaign like this.

2. Select a date for your campaign on or shortly after the official release of your book.

3. Compile a list of bonus products you will give away to each person who purchases on the designated date. Bonus products can include electronic downloads, teleseminar admission, booklets, free consulting time, and any kind of information product.

4. Contact everybody on your list and ask them to participate in your book launch campaign by agreeing to take two actions: Provide a product that you will give away as a bonus with purchase and agree to send an e-mail to their contact database on the date you've selected. Your peers should be interested in participating because this equates to free promotion for them, too. If 10 contacts send out e-mails to each of their databases, and those databases each have 10,000 subscribers, each participant has a chance to get their name in front of 100,000 people.

Here's a sample e-mail invitation:

Dear [colleague's name],

You may have heard by now that I have a new book coming out in June called *From Entrepreneur to Infopreneur: Make Money with Books, eBooks, and Information Products.* I am excited about the release of this book and am writing to **invite you to participate in a special e-mail launch campaign.**

HOW IT WORKS:

Campaign Date: June 25

I am asking you and several other industry experts to each contribute a bonus product (such as an eBook or special report) that customers will receive as a reward for purchasing my book on the campaign date. Your product will be promoted along with your name and web site link throughout the e-mail campaign thus creating tremendous exposure for you and your business!

As a campaign participant, you agree to send a special e-mail out to your mailing list on the morning of June 25 (or the evening of June 24) describing the special offer and inviting your subscribers to participate (I will send you a draft of the e-mail).

I will set up a special web page that lists all the bonus products, participants, and their web sites, and a complete description of the promotion. When a customer purchases my book from Amazon.com on June 25, he can then forward the receipt to me and I will send him the entire set of bonus products.

If you would like to contribute a product and participate in the e-mail campaign, please send me your bonus product in PDF or other format, along with a brief description of the product and its value, **no later than May 30.**

Please let me know if you have any questions. I appreciate your consideration and hope to hear from you soon.

Warm regards,
Stephanie Chandler

5. Set up a page on your web site with complete details about the special offer. Be sure to include links to web sites for each participant who contributes a product for your campaign.

6. Assemble the e-mail copy for your campaign team to use to send to their mailing list subscribers. The message should include details about the one-day only offer, a list of the bonus products readers will receive, a link to your web site page that gives a complete overview of the offer, and instructions for redeeming the offer for bonus products.

Sample E-Mail Copy

Dear Friend,

I have a special offer for you that is valid for **one day only**! My colleague, Stephanie Chandler, is releasing her powerful new book, *From Entrepreneur to Infopreneur: Make Money with Books, eBooks, and Information Products.* If you want to learn how to create information products and sell them for a profit, add revenue streams to your existing business, create products for back-of-the-room sales, or launch a new business selling information, then this is the book for you!

THE OFFER:

If you purchase this book **TODAY,** you will receive several hundred dollars worth of bonus products! Here's a list of what you will get:

- Joe Author's 32-page eBook *Marketing Mania*—a $30 value! (link to Joe's web site)
- Famous Fred's 15-page special report "Kick-Butt Sales Strategies"— a $15 value! (link to Fred's web site)
- Admission to Susie Seller's teleseminar "How to Generate Online Promotions"—worth $29.95! (link to Susie's web site)
- Annie Author's list of 500 media contacts—a $99 value! (Annie's web site)
- Edna Entrepreneur's subscription newsletter for six months— worth $29! (Edna's web site)
- Consulting time with Susie Speaker—30 minutes worth $75! (Susie's web site), etc.

How It Works:

Place your order TODAY ONLY through Amazon.com (insert link to Amazon). Forward your purchase receipt to Stephanie@businessinfoguide.com and she will send you all of these bonus products within 24 hours. It's that easy!

This is a great offer that you don't want to miss! Here is what some reviewers are saying about Stephanie's new book:

[insert endorsements]

This offer is valid for today only, so don't wait! Order your copy now. (You can thank me later!)

[insert Amazon link again]

Best regards,
Joe Participant

7. Send a reminder to your campaign team on the morning that the campaign is scheduled to occur.

8. Watch your book sales soar! Be sure to spend the day at your computer watching your sales rank improve on Amazon and delivering e-mails with bonus products for everyone who purchases your book.

STAGE THREE: AFTER THE RELEASE DATE

Once your book is finally ready, the real work begins. The early stages of a book release are critical since the mere fact that the book is new makes it newsworthy. Try doing at least one thing every day to promote your book. Even better, do two or three things every day for book promotion. These efforts will add up and will improve your chances of long-term success.

Send a Press Release

In Chapter 2, we discussed sending a press release to increase your expert status. You should also send out releases when your book is available. Try to write a captivating release with a newsworthy angle that reporters will want to cover:

Sample Press Release

FOR IMMEDIATE RELEASE

Contact: Stephanie Chandler
5800 Madison Ave., Suite W, Sacramento, CA 95841
e-mail: Stephanie@businessinfoguide.com
web site: www.businessinfoguide.com

SILICON VALLEY WORKER TRADES IN BIG PAYCHECK FOR SMALL BUSINESS AND WRITES A BOOK TO HELP OTHERS DO THE SAME

September 1, 2005, Sacramento, CA—A new business book by Stephanie Chandler, *The Business Startup Checklist and Planning Guide: Seize Your Entrepreneurial Dreams,* is the first to address the primary concerns that prevent would-be entrepreneurs from launching businesses.

According to a recent survey, a whopping 40 percent of American workers have considered starting a business but are held back by fear, funding concerns, or a lack of a business plan or idea. Chandler's book helps readers get past the fear of business ownership, decide on a business idea, formulate a plan, and locate funding.

The Business Startup Checklist and Planning Guide includes:

- A comprehensive startup checklist and planning exercises.
- Over 200 links and valuable resources including links to business license requirements for all fifty states.
- Profiles of successful entrepreneurs from the following industries: retail, specialty foods, online/Internet, franchise, real estate, pet service, child care, virtual assistance, fitness, and personal coaching.

Jay Conrad Levinson, author of the *Guerrilla Marketing* series of books, calls the book, "Mandatory reading for entrepreneurs." Romanus Wolter, author of *Kick-Start Your Dream Business* says, "Stephanie has created a valuable small business guide for anyone who wants to achieve greater success."

Chandler spent more than a decade in the Silicon Valley, but after being diagnosed with an ulcer just before her thirtieth birthday, she says, "I'd had enough. The money was no longer worth it." She opened Book Lovers Bookstore in Sacramento in 2003 and later launched a web site that provides resources for entrepreneurs: http://www.businessinfoguide.com.

The inspiration for the book and web site grew out of Chandler's frustration when launching her first business. She says, "I read dozens of business books and yet I still had unanswered questions. Not one of them gave me all of the information and resources I needed so I spent countless hours figuring things out on my own."

The research that Chandler performed led her to a new passion: helping aspiring entrepreneurs make their own dreams come true. According to Chandler, "So many people said to me, 'I wish I had the courage to do what you did.' But fear wasn't an issue for me when I left my career behind because I was so well prepared to start my business. Half the battle is proper planning."

Today Chandler is a business advisor for AllExperts.com, an instructor for SmallBiz-Bootcamp.com, has published dozens of articles, and runs two successful businesses. "Leaving corporate America was the best decision I ever made," said Chandler. "I still work just as hard, but the difference is that I love going to work every day. I want to help others realize that starting a business doesn't have to be an impossible dream."

CRAFT YOUR MEDIA PITCH

A media pitch is different from a press release because it is less formal. You can—and should—use your media pitch to contact the media directly. After you send your press release out across the wires, you should use your media pitch to contact editors and producers individually and solicit appearances.

Like a press release, your media pitch needs to be newsworthy. You need to slant your pitch as a topic of interest to a broad audience. You should also explain why the audience needs or wants this information. Your pitch should be tailored to the audience of the media source you are contacting, so you may have multiple pitches. You can e-mail, fax, or mail your pitch. The most effective way to deliver it is to pick up the phone and call.

Yes, editors and producers are busy people, but they also depend on locating interesting topics that their audiences want. Make your pitch concise and hook them with an unusual fact or statistic. When you speak to radio or television producers live, make sure you sound energetic. You want to convey how you will be an interesting and lively guest on their show. Here is an example of a media pitch to send via e-mail:

Dear [radio producer's name],

Did you know that a recent survey revealed that a whopping 40 percent of American workers have considered starting a business, but are held back from pursuing their dreams due to fear, lack of funding, or a lack of a business plan or idea?

My new book, *The Business Startup Checklist and Planning Guide: Seize Your Entrepreneurial Dreams* (Aventine Press, ISBN 1-59330-292-4, $15.95) helps ease the fears of nervous would-be entrepreneurs by providing them with all the resources they need to plan and launch a successful small business.

The resources and tools in the book are the same ones I used when I quit my six-figure job in the Silicon Valley to open Book Lovers Bookstore in Sacramento. I later went on to launch BusinessInfoGuide.com, a directory of free resources for entrepreneurs. Now my goal is to inspire others to make their dreams of entrepreneurship come true, just as I have.

I would love to be a guest on your show and give your audience tips on how to get started. I will cover the following topics:

- The easiest way to get started today
- How to overcome the fear of starting a business
- How to launch a business on a budget
- Ten easy businesses you can launch part-time or full-time
- Ten ways to promote your business at little or no cost

In addition, I will also give away five copies of the book to callers who can correctly answer questions from my fun quiz.

I hope you will agree that this will be an entertaining and informative talk for your listeners. Can we schedule something soon?

Thank you for your consideration. I look forward to hearing from you.

Best regards,
Stephanie Chandler

RADIO PROMOTION

Promoting your book on the radio is one of the best ways to reach a broad audience. The biggest advantage? You never have to leave your home. Most radio shows will gladly host guests over the telephone. Program producers are also on the lookout for guests with interesting topics.

When you schedule an engagement, offer to provide the show with a list of interview questions that you are prepared to answer. Creating this list is an excellent way to prepare your answers ahead of time and reduce your nerves. You could also offer several copies of your books as giveaways. Make it fun. Come up with a contest or quiz and give your books to people who call in with the right answer.

You can pitch your story to radio stations in several ways. You can send press releases or contact show producers individually. Show contact information and story submission procedures are listed on the web sites of the biggest shows. And the bigger the show, the better the exposure. To get the most bang for your buck, target shows that are syndicated—meaning they are broadcast to multiple markets.

Here are some other methods for getting on the air:

✔ The *Radio-Television Interview Report* is a magazine used by show producers to book guests. You can advertise in this magazine for a fee if your budget allows. Visit www.rtir.com for details.

✔ Another fee-based service is www.radiotour.com. You can be listed in their online directory, have your press release distributed to over 1,000 shows, and an e-mail sent to thousands of producers.

✔ Use the free directory on Gebbie Press (www.gebbieinc.com/radintro .htm) to locate radio stations all over the United States.

TELEVISION APPEARANCES

When pitching to television shows, it is best if you can offer something visual. TV producers love demonstrations. If you have a cookbook, offer a cooking demonstration. If you have a book on Pilates, offer to show a few exercises that viewers can do at home. You could even come up with a good story board or quiz that you can use on the air. Just make sure it's professionally designed and will look good on camera.

Pitch to TV show producers the same way you do to radio producers. Remember to make the topic interesting to a broad audience. Start by pitching to your local programs since the mere fact that you live in the region could help you secure a spot on the show. The *Today Show* and the *Oprah Winfrey Show* are the crème de la crème of talk shows; however, you should start with the smaller shows. Once you've assembled some tapes of entertaining appearances, send those—along with a captivating pitch—to the big shows.

Keep in mind that you will have to travel, most likely on your own dime, to make these show appearances. However, if you're planning to visit another city for business or vacation, mention this in your pitch. You could end with, "I will be doing a book tour in New York this November and would love to schedule an appearance on your morning show while I'm there."

To locate shows, visit their web sites or use the free directory provided by Gebbie Press: www.gebbieinc.com/tvintro.htm.

Success with Amazon.com

Amazon.com is very author and publisher friendly and allows you to add detailed content to the book description and submit information for the "Search inside This Book" program. To find out how to do this, view your book's page on Amazon and locate the link that says "Publisher: Learn how customers can search inside this book." The link should be directly below the image of the book. Be sure to investigate the Advantage and Associates programs to see which one makes the most sense for you.

Making the Best Seller List

Positions on the best seller lists are often backed by big budgets. Proven authors with big publishers often have fat budgets, media access, and promotion techniques to catapult them up the lists. But that doesn't mean a small publisher can't find the same success.

Each best seller list is tabulated differently. Most producers of lists gather their data from prominent bookstore sales. A book will often make a regional list first, which can benefit you if you live near a large market and concentrate on promoting in your area. Some authors have been known to talk their friends and family into running into prominent bookstores and buying out the inventory. This is not an easy task, but could help propel the sales numbers to noticeable heights.

Even if your title doesn't get on the best seller lists, you can still make your book a raving success. Over 100,000 new titles are published each year. If you can rally sales of just 5,000 copies in a year, your sales history will be impressive and that alone can make your book newsworthy.

REGIONAL LISTS

- ✔ *Chicago Tribune*
- ✔ *Dallas Morning News*
- ✔ *Detroit Free Press*
- ✔ *Houston Post*
- ✔ *San Francisco Chronicle*
- ✔ *Washington Post*

The following is a list of the most influential bookstores. The sales at these stores are tracked and reported to make up the best seller lists in *USA Today:*

- ✔ Books & Co. in Dayton
- ✔ Hungry Mind in St. Paul
- ✔ Kroch's & Brentano's in Chicago
- ✔ Oxford in Atlanta
- ✔ Tattered Cover in Denver
- ✔ Ingram in Nashville

MAJOR CHAINS

- ✔ Dalton
- ✔ Barnes & Noble
- ✔ Waldenbooks
- ✔ Crown
- ✔ Bookland

- ✔ Books-A-Million
- ✔ Bookstop/Bookstar
- ✔ Borders
- ✔ Brentano's
- ✔ Doubleday Book Shops
- ✔ Lauriat's
- ✔ Royal Discount Book Stores
- ✔ Scribners Bookstores

GET INTO INDEPENDENT BOOKSTORES

As a bookstore owner, I've seen it all. I get mailings, cold calls, e-mails, and author walk-ins. So which strategy works best? Without a doubt, it's the walk-in.

The walk-in gives the author a chance to make a favorable impression. Smart authors will mill around the store for awhile and then identify me as the owner because I'm handling calls and issues and appear to be in charge. When there is a break in the pace, the author will approach me with a smile and shake my hand. The conversation goes something like this: "Hi, I wanted to introduce myself. My name is Winnie Writer and I'm a local author. Are you the owner?"

I respond: "Yes, I am. I'm Stephanie Chandler. Nice to meet you." After shaking hands, the author launches into a brief pitch (the elevator-style pitch of 30 to 60 seconds) and asks some leading questions. Good questions to ask are:

- ✔ "Do you think a gardening book would be a good seller for you?"
- ✔ "Would a book that helps people get organized appeal to your customers?"
- ✔ "I noticed you have a special section for local authors. Do you think you would be interested in carrying my book?"

If the book is selling well already, it's always a good idea to mention this. If you have any media appearance scheduled, be sure to mention this, too. You could say, "I'll be on the drive-time radio program next week. I would love to tell listeners that they can get the books here."

When making a pitch, gauge the buyer's response. If she isn't immediately interested, offer to leave a copy for her to evaluate. Make sure to include an order form. It's perfectly appropriate to call back a week later to follow up, send an e-mail, or drop by again and close the deal.

If the buyer cries budget woes, then offer your book on consignment. This is nobody's favorite way to do things, but the reality is that it can get your book on the shelf and most stores are honest and fair with this practice. In my store, I accept most new books by local authors on consignment until there is a proven sales record. If a title proves it sells well, I am happy to order directly (at a 40 percent discount). I keep a simple one-page consignment agreement and have the author sign it. You should have your own agreement available just in case the store doesn't have one. Form 11.1 is the one we use.

Store managers also like autographed copies. Books that are signed often get featured on end caps or special displays. Offer to sign your books (signature only, no date). The store may have "Autographed by Author" stickers, but you should carry some with you just in case they don't.

Book Lovers Bookstore accepts _____ copies of _____
                               Quantity   Book Title

from _____ on _____. The retail
           Author Name   Date

price of the book is $_____ and the discount to Book Lovers is _____%,
                      Price   Percentage

with a total cost of $_____ per book.
              Book Lovers' Cost

Book Lovers Bookstore accepts the books on consignment and agrees to pay author for copies sold when the net due to the author exceeds $25 or quarterly if sales do not exceed $25. Book Lovers takes full responsibility for the books accepted and will pay for any shortages in inventory.

Author payments should be Payable to: _____
                                            Author or Publisher Name

And mailed to _____.
                     Mailing Address for Payments

_____   _____
Book Lovers Representative and Date   Author and Date

FORM 11.1   Book Lovers Bookstore's Book Consignment Agreement

When performing store walk-ins, make sure you have books in your car. Several authors have approached me without having any inventory with them. This makes no sense! If you want to close a deal the same day, you need to have your books ready to go. But don't lug in a case of them until you are asked. You should also have a receipt book so you can write up an invoice. Invoices are typically written as payment due at Net 30 (within 30 days). You can have invoices printed at a local print shop, or simply use blank invoices purchased from the office supply store that have your name and mailing address noted with a rubber stamp.

Since you can't walk into every store in the country, your best bet is to start locally. Your chances are better in your own backyard anyway since you have local notoriety. Then expand this practice when you travel and visit other cities.

MAILINGS

I receive hundreds of mailings, and I usually give them a quick glance. But the reality is that I don't have the time, budget, or desire to order every book that crosses my desk. As a writer, I am extrasensitive to the position that authors are in—particularly self-published authors. It's an uphill battle in a snowstorm. I would order books from them all if I only had enough resources. But I don't—and most independent stores are in the same position.

The big stores have buyers—people devoted to evaluating new books. The little guys are usually running on a skeleton staff, and buying decisions fall into the hands of an overworked store owner or manager. The good news is that nonfiction is easier to sell. We are conditioned to read fiction off the best seller list and through referrals from Oprah. With nonfiction, most readers will pick up a book because of the topic or title—not just because they read about it in *People* magazine.

I have occasionally ordered books from mailings so they aren't a complete waste of time or money. The best mailings are those that look professional and get to the point quickly. A single-page color brochure is plenty. Give yours a big, catchy headline. Remember that the buyers are scanning materials and may not read the fine print so make your point quickly. Then make it easy to place an order by including a form that lists the quantity discounts and a fax number.

Some people suggest sending a whole press kit, but in my experience, these are a waste of money. I'm not going to read through 12 pages of information. I might scan through two or three pages at the most.

Whatever you mail, make sure it sells your book. Include testimonials or snippets from book reviews. If you design your brochures yourself, make sure they look professional and have been edited. I have received some pretty unimpressive promotional materials over the years and those go straight to the circular file. With a little time and effort, you can create a captivating brochure that you can use for all kinds of book sales opportunities.

COLD CALLING

Cold calling is an option, but it may not always be the best choice. I find these calls annoying and they usually happen when I'm in the middle of something else. If you are going to call, make it quick. Try not to sound like a salesperson. You might say something like this:

"I know you're busy so I'll make this quick. My name is Annie Author and I want to introduce myself. I have a new book out called *101 Ways to Enjoy Retirement*. I will be sending you a brochure with the details and thought you would like to know that the book is already quite popular with the retirement community. Do you serve many retirees in your store?"

Ending with a question like this is perfect because it forces the buyer to answer the question—one where the answer is most likely going to be "Yes" since retirees are frequent readers. This quick call will capture the buyer's interest and the author's friendly manner will make the buyer more inclined to actually read her brochure when it arrives, preferably within a few days of the call.

E-MAIL

I don't mind e-mails from authors. In fact, I find them less intrusive than the cold call. Receiving an e-mail gives me a chance to read it and consider my response when I have the time. As with all other forms of communication, the message should be brief and to the point. Authors who compliment my store ("I visited your web site and just love the picture of your store cats!") always get extra bonus points.

E-mail costs you nothing but time so it may be an effective way to reach stores that are out of your area. To locate independent stores, check out the directories on www.booksense.com and www.bookweb.org.

Here is an example of an effective e-mail:

Subject: Author Introduction

Dear Stephanie,

I read about your store on the Internet and it looks fantastic! I am writing to introduce myself. My name is Joe Writer, and I am the author of a new book called *How to Fight the Aging Process.* According to a recent survey, three out of five people are interested in preserving their youth but don't know how to begin. My book helps readers battle aging naturally with a combination of diet, exercise, and vitamins.

Here's what some others have to say about it:

- "This book is great! It's filled with sound advice and excellent resources."—[famous author]
- "This is an impressive read. The book is written with terminology and concepts that are easy to understand. I loved it!" [book review source]

Would you be interested in ordering some copies for your store? If so, you can call (999) 999-9999 or place an order through my secure web site: www.joewriter.com. The retail price is $15.95 and the bookstore discount is 40 percent. I can also offer price breaks for orders of more than 10 copies.

Thank you very much for your consideration. Please feel free to contact me with further questions or if you would like me to send you a copy for your review.

Best regards,
Joe Writer

BOOK-SIGNING EVENTS

Scheduling a book-signing event works similarly to the way you contact independent stores and request that they carry your books. You can walk in, e-mail, or call to request an event. In this case, direct mail would probably be the least effective strategy.

To reach the big bookstores, the best tactic is to call and speak with the events coordinator. Give a quick and concise pitch for your book and explain any special presentations or gimmicks you can offer with your event. The big stores each have different policies about book signings and some may be more accommodating than others. If you are a local author, be sure to mention this since it can work to your advantage.

Make this same pitch to the smaller stores either by phone or e-mail. The store manager may want to evaluate your book first, so just comply with whatever is asked.

The mere fact that you are sitting at a table and have written a book will not cause herds of people to line up for a copy (unless you are famous). The average number of books sold at a signing event by an unknown author is six to eight copies. Most of these events are better viewed as publicity opportunities—a chance for you to get your name out there and be seen. Book signings are hard work and new authors are often disappointed by the outcome because their expectations are out of whack.

Most book signings are scheduled for two or three hours. Before you even think about setting up shop with a stack of books and a pen, you need to have a plan of action.

THE DOS AND DON'TS OF BOOK-SIGNING EVENTS

Do . . .

- ✔ Seek media coverage prior to the event. Contact local news columnists. A story in the paper or on a radio show will help with attendance.

- ✔ Send posters and bookmarks to the store one to two weeks prior to the event.

- ✔ Ask if the store would hand out bag-stuffers—small flyers that promote the event. If so, get some printed and drop them off at least two weeks prior to the event.

- ✔ Find out what kind of promotion the store offers (probably not much). Take it upon yourself to list the event with community calendars in the local paper and on www.craigslist.org.

- ✔ Tell everyone you know about it and invite them along. If you have a lot of people around you, you will attract more people who want to find out what all the fuss is about.

✔ Use props or a gimmick—anything you can bring to capture the attention of passers-by. Even a bowl of candy can help.

✔ Offer to give a talk or a presentation.

✔ Set up an eye-catching sign. It could be a picture of your book, a quiz, interesting statistics, or just a picture. Again, anything to capture interest.

✔ Smile! This is so basic, but it can be easily forgotten, especially if you're nervous. Sometimes a friendly smile and "hello" is all it takes to start a conversation with a shy customer.

✔ Be prepared to talk about your book. Plan on 5 or 10 key selling points to share when people inquire.

✔ Get up from your chair. You are not chained to that table! If you're sitting there all alone, get up and walk around. Make friendly conversation with the bookstore staff and customers.

Don't . . .

✔ Just sit there like a bump on a log. Be engaging and friendly.

✔ Wait for customers to come to you. You can go to them, or smile and welcome them to the store.

✔ Use a hard sell. Nobody wants to be guilted into buying a book. If some people say they don't read your genre, point out that Father's Day is approaching or that it makes a great holiday gift. Ask, "Do you have a relative or friend who might like a copy?"

✔ Expect the store to rally an audience for you. Some stores might list the event in their newsletter or a community calendar, but they aren't going to be your personal publicity coaches. Do the legwork and don't be disappointed if you don't have a crowd.

⚡ HOT TIP ⚡

Keep a sign-up sheet at your table during a signing event, or bring along a jar to collect business cards. Use these methods to gather contact information for your database and follow up with your newsletter or e-zine, and even a personal message of thanks for attending your event. You could even offer a free prize drawing for those who drop in a business card and give away a copy of your book or a special report.

BOOK CLUBS

Word of mouth is some of the best kind of advertising that money can't buy. Many authors have found visiting book club meetings to be a worthwhile experience. Not only does it give you a chance to connect with readers, but you get to hear valuable feedback about your book.

Though many book clubs boast a small membership (sometimes just a dozen people or less), when you make an appearance those members are bound to talk about it with their friends and family. HarperCollins Publishers believes in the value of visiting these meetings so much that it has instituted a formal program where readers can request that authors call in or visit their book club meetings.

To set this up yourself, you need to first locate book club groups and convince them to read your book. You might even offer some complimentary copies as incentive. To locate clubs in your area, inquire at local bookstores or check the Groups section of www.craigslist.org. You can also indicate on your web site that you are available to speak with book club groups. If you hear from a group outside your area, you can visit them via a conference call, which can be almost as rewarding and allows you to extend your reach.

BOOK REVIEWS

Though you sent out galley copies prior to publication for reviews in a handful of publications, once your book is available, it is worth the time and expense to send out books for possible review.

Use your media contact list to request reviews. Remember that the books section of a publication may not be the right target for you if you have published nonfiction. Keep your audience in mind and send a business book to a business editor, a parenting book to the lifestyles editor, and so on. Trade magazines can also be a good source.

If the publication doesn't list a policy for accepting books for review, it might make more sense to send a query letter first—asking if the editor is interested in receiving a copy of your book for review. You could make it easier to respond by including a postage-paid postcard or stamped envelope. Some publications will make it easy by telling you where to send a copy of your book, and some may ask for two copies.

The following example is a copy of the letter I used to contact potential reviewers:

Dear [business columnist's name],

My name is Stephanie Chandler and I have a new business book coming out this September called *The Business Startup Checklist and Planning Guide: Seize Your Entrepreneurial Dreams!* (Aventine Press, 236 pages, $15.95). I have enjoyed reading your columns and thought this book might be one you would like to read. Would you be interested in receiving a review copy?

In 2003, I fled a decade-long career in the Silicon Valley and opened Book Lovers Bookstore in Sacramento. It was the best decision I've ever made! Since then, I have launched BusinessInfoGuide.com, a directory of resources for entrepreneurs. I was inspired to write the book after I had read dozens of similar guides and was still struggling to find answers to my questions. I also heard from countless people who said, "I wish I had the courage to do what you did." It wasn't as much a matter of courage as an exercise in proper planning. Now my goal is to make it easier for others to follow their own entrepreneurial dreams!

I would love to send you a copy for review. If you would like one, please confirm your mailing address and I will get one out to you as soon as I receive my early copies (before the end of the month).

Thank you very much for your consideration!

Warm regards,
Stephanie Chandler
Book Info: www.businessinfoguide.com/book.htm

The following are some other sources to send your book for review:

✔ *Book Links* (American Library Association magazine): www.ala.org /ala/productsandpublications/periodicals/booklinks/booklinks.htm
✔ *Booklist* (American Library Association magazine): www.ala.org /ala/booklist/booklist.htm

✔ *BookPage:* www.bookpage.com

✔ *Children's Bookwatch* (Midwest Book Review): www.midwestbookreview.com/cbw

✔ *ForeWord Magazine:* www.forewordmagazine.com

✔ *Heartland Reviews:* www.heartlandreviews.com

✔ *Horn Book Magazine* (children's book reviews): www.hbook.com

✔ *Independent Publisher Magazine:* www.independentpublisher.com

✔ *Internet Bookwatch* (Midwest Book Review): www.midwestbookreview.com/ibw

✔ *Kirkus Reviews:* www.kirkusreviews.com/kirkusreviews/index.jsp

✔ *Library Journal:* www.libraryjournal.com

✔ *Library Media Connection:* www.linworth.com/lmc.html

✔ *Los Angeles Times Magazine:* www.latimes.com/features/printedition/magazine

✔ *Midwest Book Review:* www.midwestbookreview.com (they are especially considerate of independent publishers)

✔ *New York Times Book Review:* www.nytimes.com/pages/books

✔ *Publishers Weekly:* www.publishersweekly.com

✔ *School Library Journal:* www.schoollibraryjournal.com

✔ *Small Press Bookwatch* (Midwest Book Review): www.midwestbookreview.com/sbw

✔ *Small Press Review:* www.dustbooks.com/sprinfo.htm

✔ *Boston Book Review:* www.bookwire.com/bookwire/bbr/bbr-home.html

✔ *Washington Post Book World:* www.washingtonpost.com/wp-dyn/content/print/bookworld/index.html

---

⚡ HOT TIP ⚡

An online service is available that e-mails a portion of a book to members daily. Subscribers are encouraged to discuss the book online and check it out from the library or purchase it if they like what they're reading. A variety of topics are accepted for the reader service, including nonfiction and business. And the company accepts book submissions from new authors. Visit www.dearreader.com for details.

MINGLING WITH THE PROS

The industry's largest publishing trade show is Book Expo America (www.bookexpoamerica.com). All kinds of publishing industry professionals turn out for this multiday event including publishers, agents, authors, booksellers, retailers, and librarians. Book Expo America provides excellent opportunities for learning and networking.

NON-BOOKSTORE MARKETS

The sooner you can start focusing outside the bookstore, the better. Bookstores can be the worst place to sell books. Unless you can strike a deal with a store to feature your book on a special display, it is likely your book will get lost in the sea of other titles in your genre. But there are plenty of other venues for book sales.

Consider what types of businesses your book might appeal to and then call, write, or show up and make your pitch. For example, if you have a book about how to start a landscaping business, you could sell it to hardware stores and garden centers. Even if the stores don't currently carry any books, you should still approach them. Offer reasonable quantity discounts and if that doesn't work, offer to start with a consignment agreement.

Here are some other places to consider book sales opportunities:

- ✔ **Corporations**: They may buy copies to give away to employees, at conferences, for training purposes, and so on.
- ✔ **Trade associations**: Your book may be suitable to give away as a benefit of membership or for sale to members.
- ✔ **Chamber of Commerce**: Is your book a good fit as a giveaway to members or to sell to the general public?
- ✔ **Colleges**: The textbook market is always eager for new books. They may use your book as is or rebind it in their own imprint.
- ✔ **Catalogs**: Thousands of mail-order catalogs are distributed each year. Contact buyers in catalogs where you think your book is a good

fit. For a list of catalog directories, visit www.businessinfoguide
.com/catalogs.htm.

✔ **Home shopping channels:** Book sales have steadily increased on
home shopping sites. Check out QVC's submission process at
www.qvcproductsearch.com.

✔ **eBay:** Though you probably won't sell thousands of books on eBay,
you can use the auction site to get rid of damaged copies or even
perfectly clean copies. It costs just a fraction of the sales price to
sell on eBay and the added advantage is the exposure you will bring
to your title. Millions of people visit eBay every day and even if they
don't buy your book, those who see it will remember it and may
buy it later from eBay or a bookstore.

✔ **Local businesses:** Got a title that would appeal to the audience at
a local gift shop or restaurant? Look around your area to identify
where your target market is shopping, then approach the business
owners or buyers and offer your title. If they resist, offer it on consignment and test the market. You can provide an inexpensive, attractive display, and if your books sell well, you can bet the buyer
will be happy to convert your agreement from consignment to direct purchase.

PARTY TIME

Be sure to throw yourself a big book launch party! This is your chance to celebrate your success with your family, friends, and possibly even the media.
Consider holding your event at a local bookstore, restaurant, office building,
or retail shop with a theme related to your book. A public venue is a good
choice since you can draw attention from passersby.

You could have the event catered or simply spring for some appetizers
or dessert. Invite everyone you know—family, friends, business associates,
peers—and encourage each person to bring a friend. Also send invitations to
the local media—the evening news might need a filler piece and your timing
could be perfect.

Make your book available for sale at the back of the room and offer to
autograph copies. Be sure to give a brief speech to thank everyone for coming and talk a bit about how the book came to fruition. Give away bookmarks and postcards and any other reminders of your book. Ask guests to

sign up for your mailing list. I attended a launch party where the author had a computer set up so that attendees could easily post a review for his book on Amazon.com right there at the event.

Think of ways to make your launch party fun and memorable. It's your day to shine. Don't feel shy about holding an event like this. The people who love you most will want to support you and everyone else will be thrilled to be invited to such a unique event. Remember to take pictures to add to your web site and possibly use as publicity photos and most importantly, have a wonderful time!

ADDITIONAL RESOURCES

- *Jump Start Your Book Sales* by Tom and Marilyn Ross
- *1001 Ways to Market Your Books* by John Kremer
- *Beyond the Bookstore: How to Sell More Books Profitably to NonBookstore Markets* by Brian Jud

Infopreneur Profile

Susan Harrow
Harrow Communications
Oakland, California
www.prsecrets.com

PUBLICATIONS:

- *Sell Yourself without Selling Your Soul: A Woman's Guide to Promoting Herself, Her Business, Her Product, or Her Cause with Integrity and Spirit* (trade paperback, HarperCollins, $15.95)
- *Get a Six Figure Book Advance* (eBook, $197.00; ring-bound book additional $39.00 with eBook purchase only)
- *The Ultimate Guide to Getting Booked on Oprah: Ten Steps to Becoming a Guest on the World's Top Talk Show* (ring-bound book or eBook, $99.00)
- *Oprah Show Tips* (3-CD set, $59.95; co-produced with Joan Stewart)

- *Oprah Training Kit* (ring-bound book, eBook, and CD bundle, $147.00)
- *Skyrocket Your Speaking and Writing Career* (eBook, $29.95)
- *Speak at the Learning Annex® and Adult Learning Centers to Skyrocket Your Consulting, Coaching and Product Sales* (CD and Transcript $49.90)
- *Best Seller: Turn Your Book into a Best Seller in Less Than 6 Hours* (4-cassette or CD series, $59.95)
- *Secrets to Getting Top TV Show Producers to Book You as Their Guest* (eBook, $19.95)
- *Super Saver Bundle* (many of Susan's products for $247.00)

Who is your target audience for your materials?

Primarily entrepreneurs, work-at-home moms, and speakers. I get a lot of authors and people who want to be authors. Women really respond as well as people who are more socially conscious and spiritually oriented.

The way that I wanted to differentiate myself in my market was to avoid talking about sports, sex, or using sales or PR jargon. My book (*Sell Yourself without Selling Your Soul*) is not overtly spiritual, but it's woven through.

In a way it's a lifestyle book. It integrates life and work and family and everything—everything needs to be in complete congruence. People have used it for everything from a parenting guide to a relationship guide. It's working in all kinds of mysterious ways.

How did you begin your infopreneur business?

Years ago I was teaching at the Learning Annex [in San Francisco] and saw a booklet that another instructor was selling. So I wrote my own booklet on how to write a press release packet and started selling it to the students. It was about 20 pages and I think I sold it for around $10.00. Later, it became a chapter in *Sell Yourself*.

I also had the foresight to tape every talk that I gave. I had them reproduced on cassettes and started selling those, too. Then some guy from one of my classes said, "You're selling your stuff too cheap. You could get a lot more for your materials." So I started raising my prices from $12.00

to $15.00 and so on. People still bought my stuff even with higher prices. There is a perceived value when you pay more.

Where do you sell your products?

Through my web site and back-of-the-room sales when I speak. I also have an affiliate program that allows other people to promote and sell my products. You really need to support your affiliates [if you want them to sell for you]. It's important to keep the needs of the affiliates in mind—it's the same philosophy as when you're working with a producer. You want to do all the work for them. So I make sales copy for my products available to affiliates in different lengths. That way they have several different versions of copy to fit their needs.

I also use autoresponders extensively. I use them to send tips and reminders to people who have bought my products. It took a lot of time to set them up but I do feel like they've made a difference in my sales. My goal this year is to make $100K in passive income and part of that strategy is using autoresponders. They make people feel like I'm writing to them personally—and in a way, I am.

You're published with a major publishing house. How did you secure your book deal?

Patti Breitman heard me speak—she's the literary agent for John Gray (*Men Are from Mars*) and Richard Carlson (*Don't Sweat the Small Stuff*)—at a NCBPMA [Northern California Book Publicity and Marketing Association] meeting. This woman was asking questions and I noticed her because she was so bright eyed. When I found out who she was, I introduced myself and told her I had an idea for an illustrated book and asked if she would be my agent. She said she didn't do illustrated books. Then she asked about my consulting rates for some of her clients—I charge $500 per hour—and she said I was too expensive.

A few months later I had another speaking engagement for the Authors Guild and Patti was there with two clients she wanted to be publicity savvy. Before I spoke, the organizer went around the room asked about everybody's new book ideas. We each gave a 20-second pitch. So I rattled off a pitch for *Sell Yourself without Selling Your Soul,* and at the end of my talk, Patti said she loved my generosity of spirit and subject matter. She said that if I were to write a proposal, then she would consider representing me. Three proposals and nine months later, we had a book deal with HarperCollins.

Most big publishing houses only want authors who have big platforms. How did you convince HarperCollins that you had a large enough platform?

I had been teaching at the Learning Annex [in San Francisco] so I had a small platform. I had a newsletter list and the start of some prestigious clients. Since the book was on publicity, I guess they assumed I knew how to do it! We thought it would get six figures and it didn't—partly because I didn't have a large enough platform.

How does a new author develop a large enough platform to get the big publishers interested?

You have to have a presence in the world and your voice needs to be heard in as many venues as possible: Internet, magazines, newspapers, radio, television. You need to be out there giving seminars, blogging, and podcasting. It's important because what people don't understand about publicity is that it requires those 7 or 20 impressions over time. Often they need to see your name everywhere before they trust you and buy your products.

How do you work with your clients? What advice do you give them?

I have three different questionnaires that I use with my clients. I ask questions like How do you want to grow your business? What are your monetary goals? What things do you love to do most? How do you want to spend your time? Then we map out a plan and put a time line around it.

   If my client wants to be on the radio, for example, I ask, "What do you want to happen from your radio appearance? Do you want to book speaking engagements, have people go to your web site to buy books, get clients? What are your overall goals in everything you do?" Then I remind them that it has to be customer oriented. You have to consider how you are bringing value to that audience.

For example, I recently spoke to an audience of athletes. Since I have a background as a tennis pro, I used sports analogies in my talk. See what I mean?

Looking back, is there anything you would do differently?

I would have realized that there is really no price difference between $19.95 and $39.95—it's all in the perceived value. I would have started bundling my products together sooner. Some people want to buy everything you have! And I would have had all of my autoresponders set up before I began promoting a product. I want my customers to feel like I'm holding their hand—like I'm with them every step of the way. Now I have that.

CHAPTER

12

Carpe Diem:
Put Your Plans
into Action

Bite off more than you can chew, then chew it. Plan more than you can do, then do it.

—ANONYMOUS

Though the ideas and stories in this book may get your wheels spinning, be careful not to take on too many projects at once. This is sure to sabotage your info products strategy. Many entrepreneurs fall into the trap of trying to do too much at once. Instead, prioritize your goals and tackle them one at a time.

When determining your info product strategy, first decide where your strengths and interests lie. Are you a good writer? Then books and eBooks may be a good place to start. Do your friends compare you to a radio personality? Then audio programs or teleseminars may be for you.

Just as you would create a business plan for a new business, it's a good idea to map out a plan for your information product success. Include your goals and a targeted time line to keep you on track, and don't worry too much if your strategy changes as you go along. Just make sure you are moving forward and making things happen.

You can use the following outline to plan out your strategy. Add or eliminate topics to fit the needs of your situation:

INFORMATION PRODUCT PLAN CHECKLIST

❑ **Design and launch a web site.**
  ❑ Hire a designer or select software for site design.
  ❑ Select a hosting provider and register a domain name.
  ❑ Implement search engine optimization techniques.
  ❑ Submit site to search engines.
  ❑ Begin online marketing campaign.

❑ **Send a monthly newsletter or e-zine.**
  ❑ Set up a form to capture subscribers from your web site.
  ❑ Develop a giveaway product to reward new subscribers.
  ❑ Outline content to include in newsletters.
  ❑ Solicit contributions for newsletter content.

❑ **Begin keeping a journal or notebook with product ideas.**
  ❑ Jot down new ideas as they come to you.
  ❑ Create separate sections for product ideas and marketing ideas.

❑ **Decide which line of products to develop first.**
  ❑ Develop a time line for launching your first three products.
  ❑ Outline the topics and process for your first info product.
  ❑ Begin developing your product.
  ❑ Set a price for your product.
  ❑ Evaluate and implement a shopping cart or payment collection service.
  ❑ Launch the product with fanfare and by following your marketing strategy.

❑ **Develop your marketing campaign.**
  ❑ Make a list of marketing strategies you plan to implement.
  ❑ Do three to five things each day to market your business and product.
  ❑ Test out what works and doesn't work. Repeat strategies that work best.

❑ **Continue the product development cycle.**
  ❑ Evaluate product sales and response to marketing efforts.

❏ Test different pricing strategies if yours isn't working.

❏ Continue developing products and following your checklist.

Don't forget to have fun with your products and with your infopreneur business. It may be a serious business, but it should also be one that you enjoy. Life is always more interesting when pursued with passion. You can quote me on that!

Infopreneur Profile

Shel Horowitz
Accurate Writing & More/AWM Books
Hadley, Massachusetts
www.principledprofits.com, www.frugalmarketing.com,
www.frugalfun.com

PUBLICATIONS:

- *Principled Profit: Marketing That Puts People First* (trade paperback, $17.50; guide to success through ethical, cooperative business principles, especially as applied in marketing.)
- *The Penny-Pinching Hedonist: How to Live Like Royalty with a Peasant's Pocketbook* (eBook, $8.50; how to have fun cheaply.)

Who is your target audience for your materials?

- Business owners and managers who want to do the right thing, but battle the perception that you have to be a bad guy to succeed.
- Frugal people who want more joy in their lives; big spenders who want to save money while still enjoying live entertainment, exotic vacations, fine dining, and so on.

Where do you sell your materials?

Web sites (one per book), online discussion groups, back of the room at speeches, special sales, resellers, and through a distributor.

When did you first publish your material?
A. 2003.
B. 1995.

What made you decide to self-publish?
I wanted a fast timetable and full control. My agent approached 30 publishers. It was self-publish or not publish (I have also published three books with traditional publishers).

How does your publication enhance your business?
A few among many ways:

- My book on business ethics and my nonself-published books on frugal marketing continue to open many doors. The direct income stream from the books is not that large, but many people buy the book(s) and then hire me for anything from a $145 press release or consultation on up to full shepherding and extensive marketing of their book, or ongoing marketing of their products and services, spending several thousand dollars with me. Others are aware of the books and are influenced to buy my services without even reading the books first.
- My experience as a successful publisher enables me to consult other would-be publishers, and that is turning into a significant component of my business.
- Being the author of two award-winning books (one self-pubbed, one traditionally published) is a passport to speaking gigs. It also makes me a much more desirable interview subject and book contributor.
- The passive income stream from converting my out-of-print book to an eBook has been a nice residual for a book that, by traditional approaches, had already paid its way and was finished. It turned out to be very timely; within weeks of the conversion, the book was featured on MSN's home page. Not only did I sell 60 eBooks from that single story, but that month I got a very fat check from Google for advertising commissions. Also, by keeping the book available, I can continue to get press for it. Since going out of

print, the book has been on MSN at least three times, *Woman's Day, Reader's Digest,* and so on, plus numerous radio shows.

- My most recent self-pubbed book, *Principled Profit: Marketing That Puts People First,* was profitable on the day presses rolled, thanks to a corporate sale of 1,000 copies. So there was zero downside. I've also pursued foreign rights and am currently negotiating my third sale (India and Mexico are complete, and Nigeria is in process).
- Buying back my book, *Marketing without Megabucks: How to Sell Anything on a Shoestring,* from Simon & Schuster, was the single key factor in going from a small locally based shop to a national and international consulting and copywriting business—because it got me involved in Internet discussion lists.

What was the process you used to publish?

I started a publishing company and first self-published in 1985, did everything wrong imaginable, but somehow still broke even. That book was revised and expanded into my Simon & Schuster book. For my 1995 book, I read several of the books, did much of the production and design work myself, and made a lot of mistakes.

In 1996, I joined the first of several Internet discussion lists for small publishers/self-publishers, and as a result, was much better educated. This gave me leverage to create a very unusual contract when Chelsea Green brought out an expanded and updated version of MWM, *Grassroots Marketing: Getting Noticed in a Noisy World* (e.g., I have the nonexclusive right to sell foreign rights). My third time at bat with self-publishing, in 2003, I hired interior and cover designers, an indexer, and a copyeditor. I entered several awards and won a few.

How do you market your materials?

For *Principled Profit,* I engaged in two relationship-based campaigns along the lines that I recommend in the book, enabling me to crack the Amazon Top 100 (going from 1,558,475 to number 83 overall and number 12 in the business category, and without offering bonuses) and launch the Ethics Pledge campaign (of which 20 to 25 percent of signers buy the book) through extensive publicity in various Internet newsletters, blogs, and web sites.

I also have a dedicated web site on the theme of each of my most recent three books.

When I speak, I expect to sell a goodly number of books.

What has been the most challenging part of the publishing process?

Knowing all the things I should do, but lacking the time and money to carry them out.

What has been the most rewarding part of the publishing process?

Making a difference in people's lives, and in the world climate, by sharing life-changing ideas, strategies, and tactics.

What have you learned from the experience that you would like to share with others?

That the independent publishing community is populated with generous, helpful, fascinating people, and collectively, they have expertise on absolutely everything.

Looking back, is there anything you would do differently?

Lots. For *The Penny-Pinching Hedonist: How to Live Like Royalty with a Peasant's Pocketbook,* I'd have joined the online publishing group six months before publication instead of six months after, and as a result, would have produced a book with higher production values, a lower price, and a better title.

For *Principled Profit: Marketing That Puts People First* I'd have gon a bit slower, made several strategic changes in my Amazon campaign, pushed harder on foreign and book club rights, and maybe printed enough copies to make bookstores a viable channel. And I still need to figure out how to make this book appeal more to mainstream media and mainstream booksellers.

—— Directory of Resources ——

✔ WEB SITES FOR PROFILED INFOPRENEURS

Tom Antion: www.antion.com.

C. Hope Clark: www.fundsforwriters.com.

Michelle Dunn: www.michelledunn.com and www.credit-and-collections
.com.

Alyice Edrich: www.thedabblingmum.com.

Paulette Ensign: www.tipsbooklets.com.

Susan Harrow: www.prsecrets.com.

Shel Horowitz: www.principledprofits.com, www.frugalmarketing.com, www
.frugalfun.com.

Dan Poynter: www.parapublishing.com.

Joan Stewart: www.publicityhound.com.

Dottie Walters: www.speakandgrowrich.com.

Romanus Wolter: www.kickstartguy.com.

✔ RESOURCES FOR PROFESSIONAL SPEAKING

BusinessInfoGuide: www.businessinfoguide.com/speaking.htm.

Jokes: www.jokes.com.

The Jokes: www.the-jokes.com.

Learning Annex: www.learningannex.com.

National Speakers Association: www.nsaspeaker.org.

Never Be Boring Again by Doug Stevenson, published by Cornelia Press, 2004.

Professional Speakers Association: www.professionalspeakers.org.

Speak and Grow Rich by Dottie Walters, published by Prentice Hall Press,
1997.

Speaker Match: www.speakermatch.com.

SpeakerNetNews: http://speakernetnews.com.

Toastmasters: www.toastmasters.com.

World Class Speakers and Entertainers: www.speak.com.

✔ TRADE ASSOCIATIONS FOR WRITERS

American Society of Journalists and Authors: www.asja.org.

Arizona Book Publishing Association: www.azbookpub.com.

Association of Authors and Publishers: www.authorsandpublishers.org.

Bay Area Independent Publishers Association: www.baipa.org.

Book Publishers Northwest: www.bpnw.org.

Colorado Independent Publishers Association: www.cipabooks.com.

Connecticut Authors and Publishers Association: www.aboutcapa.com.

Directory and Database Publishers Forum & Network: www.dpfn.com.

Florida Publishers Association: www.flbookpub.org.

Illinois Women's Press Association: www.iwpa.org.

Independent Writers of Southern California: www.iwosc.org.

Minnesota Book Publishers Round Table: www.publishersroundtable.org.

National Association of Women Writers: www.nationalwriters.com.

National Writers Association: www.nationalwriters.com.

New Mexico Book Association: www.nmbook.org.

Northern California Publishers & Authors: www.norcalpa.org.

Publishers Association of the South: www.pubsouth.org.

St. Louis Publishers Association: www.stlouispublishers.org.

Small Publishers, Artists, and Writers Network: www.spawn.org.

Wisconsin Regional Writers Association: www.wrwa.net.

Writers League of Texas: www.writersleague.org.

✔ WRITERS' RESOURCES

Absolute Write: www.absolutewrite.com.

Bird by Bird: Some Instructions on Writing and Life by Anne Lamott, published by Anchor, 1995.

The Classic Guide to Better Writing: Step-by-Step Techniques and Exercises to Write Simply, Clearly and Correctly by Rudolph Flesch, published by HarperCollins, 50th anniversary edition, 1996.

Freelance Success: www.freelancesuccess.com.

Funds for Writers: www.fundsforwriters.com.

Media Bistro: www.mediabistro.com.

On Writing Well: The Classic Guide to Writing Nonfiction by William Zinsser, published by HarperCollins, 30th anniversary edition, 2006.

Poets & Writers Magazine: www.pw.org.

Shaw Guides: http://writing.shawguides.com.

The Writer Magazine: www.writermag.com.

Writers Digest: www.writersdigest.com.

Writers Market: www.writersmarket.com.

Writers Net: www.writers.net.

Writers Weekly: www.writersweekly.com.

✔ RESOURCES FOR FINDING LITERARY AGENTS

The Association of Authors Representatives: www.aar-online.org/mc/page .do.

Jeff Herman's Book of Publishers, Editors, and Literary Agents by Jeff Herman, published by Three Dog Press, 2005, 16th edition.

Predators and Editors: www.anotherealm.com/prededitors.

Publisher's Marketplace: www.publishersmarketplace.com.

Writer's Market by Kathryn S. Brogan, Robert Lee Brewer, and Joanna Masterson, published by Writer's Digest Books, 2005.

✔ RESOURCES FOR WRITING A BOOK PROPOSAL

Absolute Write (sample book proposal): www.absolutewrite.com/novels /book_proposal1.htm.

Guerrilla Marketing for Writers: 100 Weapons to Help You Sell Your Work by Jay Conrad Levinson, Michael Larsen, and Rick Frishman, published by Writer's Digest Books, 2000.

How to Write a Book Proposal by Michael Larsen, published by Writer's Digest Books, 2004, 3rd edition.

Write the Perfect Book Proposal: 10 Proposals That Sold and Why by Jeff Herman and Deborah Levine Herman, published by John Wiley & Sons, 2001, 2nd edition.

✔ RESOURCES FOR PUBLISHING

Bar Code Graphics: www.createbarcodes.com.

Bar code providers list: www.isbn.org/standards/home/isbn/us/barcode.asp.

Beyond the Bookstore: How to Sell More Books Profitably to Non-Bookstore Markets by Brian Jud, published by Reed Press, 2003.

Book Locker (print on demand publisher of books and eBooks): www.booklocker.com.

Book Market (list of book distributors): www.bookmarket.com/distributors .html.

Book Market (list of book printers): www.bookmarket.com/101print.html.

Book Promotion Newsletter: www.bookpromotionnewsletter.com.

Book Zone Pro (list of book distributors): www.bookzonepro.com/resources/morelinks/distwhole.html.

Bowker (issues ISBN numbers): www.bowker.com.

Business Info Guide: www.BusinessInfoGuide.com/publishing.htm.

Copyright your work: www.copyright.gov.

Jump Start Your Book Sales: A Money-Making Guide for Authors, Independent Publishers and Small Presses by Tom and Marilyn Ross, published by Writer's Digest Books, 1999.

Library of Congress: http://pcn.loc.gov.

Lulu (print on demand publisher): www.lulu.com.

1001 Ways to Market Your Books by John Kremer, published by Open Horizons, 2000.

Para Publishing: www.ParaPublishing.com.

Publishers Marketing Association: www.pmaonline.org.

Publish on Demand: www.PublishonDemand.net.

The Self-Publishing Manual by Dan Poynter, published by Para Publishing, 2003, 14th edition.

Small Publishers Association of North America: www.spannet.org.

Tips Booklets: www.tipsbooklets.com.

✔ RESOURCES FOR BOOK REVIEWS

Amazon: Editorial Department, Category Editor (e.g., Travel Editor), Amazon .com, 705 Fifth Ave South, 5th floor, Seattle, WA 98104.

Book Links (American Library Association magazine): www.ala.org/ala /productsandpublications/periodicals/booklinks/booklinks.htm.

Booklist (American Library Association magazine): www.ala.org/ala/booklist /booklist.htm.

BookPage: www.bookpage.com.

Boston Book Review: www.bookwire.com/bookwire/bbr/bbr-home.html.

Children's Bookwatch (Midwest Book Review): www.midwestbookreview .com/cbw.

ForeWord Magazine: www.forewordmagazine.com.

Heartland Reviews: www.heartlandreviews.com.

Horn Book Magazine (children's book reviews): www.hbook.com.

Independent Publisher Magazine: www.independentpublisher.com.

Internet Bookwatch (Midwest Book Review): www.midwestbookreview .com/ibw.

Kirkus Reviews: www.kirkusreviews.com/kirkusreviews/index.jsp.

Library Journal: www.libraryjournal.com.

Library Media Connection: www.linworth.com/lmc.html.

Los Angeles Times Magazine: www.latimes.com/features/printedition /magazine.

Midwest Book Review: www.midwestbookreview.com (especially considerate of independent publishers).

New York Times Book Review: www.nytimes.com/pages/books.

Publishers Weekly: www.publishersweekly.com.

School Library Journal: www.schoollibraryjournal.com.

Small Press Bookwatch (Midwest Book Review): www.midwestbookreview
.com/sbw.

Small Press Review: www.dustbooks.com/sprinfo.htm.

Washington Post Book World: www.washingtonpost.com/wp-dyn/content
/print/bookworld/index.html.

✔ EBOOK PUBLISHING

Activ eBook Compiler: www.ebookcompiler.com.

Adobe Acrobat (PDF creator): www.adobe.com.

Adobe Reader: www.adobe.com/products/acrobat/readstep2.html.

Desktop Author: www.desktopauthor.com.

eBook Edit Pro: www.ebookedit.com.

eBook Generator: www.ebookgenerator.com.

eBook Mall: www.ebookmall-publishing.com.

eBooks 'N Bytes: www.ebooksnbytes.com.

eCover Creator: www.logocreator.com.

eCover Generator: www.ecovergenerator.com.

Hiebook Reader: www.hiebook.com.

Lightning Source (LSI): www.LightningSource.com.

Microsoft Reader: www.microsoft.com/reader/developers/downloads/rmr.asp.

Mobipocket Reader: www.mobipocket.com.

Palm Reader: http://ebooks.palm.com/product/detail/19286.

Payloadz: www.payloadz.com.

Yahoo Group for eBook Publishing: http://groups.yahoo.com/group
/ebook-community.

✔ LOCATE FREELANCE WRITERS/GHOST WRITERS/GRAPHIC ARTISTS

All Freelance: www.allfreelancework.com.

Craigslist: www.craigslist.org.

Elance: www.elance.com.

Freelance Success: www.freelancesuccess.com.

Publishers Marketplace: www.publishersmarketplace.com.

✔ ONLINE ARTICLE DISTRIBUTION SERVICES

Amazines: www.amazines.com.

Article Alley: www.articlealley.com.

Article City: www.articlecity.com.

Ezine Articles: www.ezinearticles.com.

Idea Marketers: www.ideamarketers.com.

✔ PRESS RELEASES

Business Wire: www.businesswire.com.

EReleases: www.ereleases.com.

Free Press Release: www.free-press-release.com.

PR News Wire: www.prnewswire.com.

PRWeb: www.prweb.com.

Xpress Press: www.xpresspress.com.

✔ PUBLICITY AND PUBLIC RELATIONS

Annie Jennings PR: www.anniejenningspr.com.

Gebbie Press (list of radio stations): www.gebbieinc.com/radintro.htm.

Gebbie Press (list of TV stations): www.gebbieinc.com/tvintro.htm.

Joan Stewart's Site: www.publicityhound.com.

PR Leads: www.prleads.com.

Radio Tour: www.radiotour.com.

Radio TV Interview Report: www.rtir.com.

Susan Harrow's Site: www.prsecrets.com.

✔ TELECONFERENCE SERVICE PROVIDERS

Audio Acrobat (recording technology): http://www.audioacrobat.com.

Budget Conferencing: www.budgetconferencing.com.

Conference Call.com: www.conferencecall.com.

Free Conference Call: www.freeconferencecall.com.

Great Teleseminars: www.greatteleseminars.com.

✔ WEB CONFERENCING RESOURCES

Lifesize: www.lifesize.com.

WebEx: www.webex.com.

✔ FORUM SERVICE PROVIDERS

BulletinBoards.com: www.bulletinboards.com.

Phorum: www.phorum.org.

PHPBB: www.phpbb.com.

World Crossing: http://wc0.worldcrossing.com.

✔ FORUMS

About.com: www.entrepreneurs.about.com/mpboards.htm.

Business Know How: www.businessknowhow.com/forum.

Business Owner's Idea Cafe: www.businessownersideacafe.com
/cyberschmooz.

Internet Based Moms site: http://Internetbasedmoms.com/bb.

LinkedIn: www.linkedin.com.

Minding Your Own Business: http://myob-network.ryze.com.

Ryze: www.ryze.com.

The Small Business Forum: www.small-business-forum.com.

Yahoo Groups: http://groups.yahoo.com.

✔ COMPUTER-BASED TRAINING

Custom Guide: www.customguide.com/index.htm.

Epath Learning: www.epathlearning.com.

Trigent: www.trigent.com.

✔ RESOURCES FOR AUDIO AND VIDEO PRODUCTION

Cassette Works: www.m2com.com/cassetteworks.html.

Fed Ex/Kinkos: www.fedex.com/us/officeprint/main.

VCorp: www.vcorp99.com.

Video Project Studio: www.videoprojectstudio.com.

✔ DICTATION SOFTWARE

Dictation Buddy (dictation software): www.highcriteria.com.

Naturally Speaking (dictation software): www.nuance.com.

✔ WEB SITE HOSTING, DESIGN, AND MANAGEMENT

American Author: www.americanauthor.com.

Frontpage Resource: http://accessfp.net.

Geocities (web hosting): http://geocities.yahoo.com.

Go Daddy (web hosting): www.godaddy.com.

Google Ad Words (paid ads): www.google.com.

Network Solutions (web hosting): www.networksolutions.com.

1Shopping Cart (shopping cart and autoresponders): www.1shoppingcart .com.

Overture (pay for placement): www.overture.com.

Pay Dot Com (affiliate program): www.paydotcom.com.

Payloadz (shopping cart for electronic documents): www.payloadz.com.

Paymentech (merchant card processing): www.paymentech.net.

Paypal (merchant card processing and shopping cart): www.paypal.com.

The Template Store: www.thetemplatestore.com.

Whois (domain ownership information): www.internic.net/whois.html.

Yahoo (domains): www.smallbusiness.yahoo.com/domains.

Yahoo (merchant solutions): http://smallbusiness.yahoo.com
   /merchant.

Yahoo (web hosting): www.smallbusiness.yahoo.com.

✔ NEWSLETTER TECHNOLOGY PROVIDERS/AUTORESPONDERS

Constant Contact: www.constantcontact.com.

EZEzine: www.ezezine.com.

1Shopping Cart: www.1shoppingcart.com.

Zinester: www.zinester.com.

✔ SUBMIT TO SEARCH ENGINES

Addme: http://tools.addme.com/servlet/s0new.

Entireweb: http://addurl.entireweb.com/main.php.

Free Web Submission: www.freewebsubmission.com.

Google: www.google.com/addurl.html.

Google's Froogle Merchant Program: www.google.com/froogle/merchants
   /apply.

Info Tiger: www.infotiger.com/addurl.html.

MSN: http://beta.search.msn.com/docs/submit.aspx.

Nerd World: www.nerdworld.com/nwadd.html.

Open Directory Project: http://dmoz.org/add.html.

Subjex: www.subjex.net/submit_url.html.

Submit Net (paid submissions): www.submitnet.net.

Yahoo: http://submit.search.yahoo.com/free/request.

✔ BOOKSTORES

Amazon: www.amazon.com.
Barnes & Noble: www.barnesandnoble.com.
Booksense: www.booksense.com.
Bookweb: www.bookweb.org.

✔ SHIPPING SERVICE PROVIDERS

Federal Express: www.fedex.com.
Papermart (supplies): www.papermart.com.
Ship SMO (fulfillment service): www.shipsmo.com.
Small Business Warehousing (fulfillment service): www.sbwarehousing.com.
Specialty Fulfillment Center (fulfillment service): www.pickandship.com.
Uline (supplies): www.uline.com.
United Parcel Service: www.ups.com.
U.S. Post Office: www.usps.gov.

✔ BLOG SERVICE PROVIDERS

Blog Critics: www.blogcritics.com.
Blogger: www.blogger.com.
Blogs for Small Business (directory): www.blogsforsmallbusiness.com.
Globe of Blogs: www.globeofblogs.com.
Live Journal: www.livejournal.com.
Tripod: www.tripod.lycos.com.
Typepad: www.typepad.com.

✔ PRINTING SERVICES

iPrint: www.iPrint.com.
Got Print: www.GotPrint.com.
VistaPrint: www.VistaPrint.com.

✔ ONLINE ARTICLES

Amazines: www.amazines.com.

Article Alley: www.articlealley.com.

Article City: www.articlecity.com.

Ezine Articles: www.ezinearticles.com.

Idea Marketers: www.ideamarketers.com.

✔ NEWSPAPERS

Miami Herald: www.miami.com/mld/miamiherald.

New York Times: www.nytimes.com.

San Francisco Chronicle: http://sfgate.com/chronicle.

Washington Post: www.washingtonpost.com.

USA Today: www.usatoday.com.

✔ MISCELLANEOUS RESOURCES

All Experts: www.allexperts.com.

Chase's Calendar of Events: http://books.mcgraw-hill.com/getpage
   .php?page=chases_intro.php&template=chases.

Craigslist (community calendar): www.craigslist.org.

Dear Reader (reader service): www.dearreader.com.

International Virtual Assistants Association: www.ivaa.org.

List of catalog directories: www.businessinfoguide.com/catalogs.htm.

Microsoft (newsletter templates): http://office.microsoft.com/en-us/templates
   /default.aspx.

Perform a trademark search: www.uspto.gov.

QVC (product search): www.qvcproductsearch.com.

✔ BUSINESS LICENSE RESOURCES BY STATES

Alabama: www.ador.state.al.us/licenses/authrity.html.

Alaska: www.dced.state.ak.us/occ/buslic.htm.

Arizona: www.revenue.state.az.us/license.htm.

Arkansas: www.state.ar.us/online_business.php.

California: www.calgold.ca.gov.

Colorado: www.state.co.us/gov_dir/obd/blid.htm.

Connecticut: www.state.ct.us.

Delaware: www.state.de.us/revenue/obt/obtmain.htm.

District of Columbia: www.dcra.dc.gov.

Florida: http://sun6.dms.state.fl.us/dor/businesses.

Georgia: www.sos.state.ga.us/corporations/regforms.htm.

Hawaii: www.hawaii.gov/dbedt/start/starting.html.

Idaho: www.idoc.state.id.us/Pages/BUSINESSPAGE.html.

Illinois: www.sos.state.il.us/departments/business_services/business.html.

Indiana: www.state.in.us/sic/owners/ia.html.

Iowa: www.iowasmart.com/blic.

Kansas: www.accesskansas.org/businesscenter/index.html?link=start.

Kentucky: www.thinkkentucky.com/kyedc/ebpermits.asp.

Louisiana: www.sec.state.la.us/comm/fss/fss-index.htm.

Maine: www.econdevmaine.com/biz-develop.htm.

Maryland: www.dllr.state.md.us.

Massachusetts: www.state.ma.us/sec/cor/coridx.htm.

Michigan: http://medc.michigan.org/services/startups/index2.asp.

Minnesota: www.dted.state.mn.uss.

Mississippi: www.olemiss.edu/depts/mssbdc/going_intobus.html.

Missouri: www.ded.state.mo.us/business/businesscenter.

Montana: www.state.mt.us/sos/biz.htm.

Nebraska: www.nebraska.gov/business/html/337/index.phtml.

Nevada: www.nv.gov.

New Hampshire: www.nhsbdc.org/startup.htm.

New Jersey: www.state.nj.us/njbiz/s_lic_and_cert.shtml.

New Mexico: http://edd.state.nm.us/NMBUSINESS.

New York: www.dos.state.ny.us/lcns/licensing.html.

North Carolina: www.secstate.state.nc.us/secstate/blio/default.htm.

North Dakota: www.state.nd.us/sec.

Ohio: www.state.oh.us/sos/business_services_information.htm.

Oklahoma: www.okonestop.com.

Oregon: www.filinginoregon.com.

Pennsylvania: www.paopenforbusiness.state.pa.us.

Rhode Island: www.corps.state.ri.us/firststop/index.asp.

South Carolina: www.state.sd.us/STATE/sitecategory.cfm?mp=Licenses
/Occupations.

South Dakota: www.sd.gov/Main_Login.asp.

Tennessee: www.state.tn.us/ecd/res_guide.htm.

Texas: www.tded.state.tx.us/guide.

Utah: www.commerce.state.ut.us/web/commerce/admin/licen.htm.

Vermont: www.sec.state.vt.us.

Virginia: www.dba.state.va.us/licenses.

Washington: www.wa.gov/dol/bpd/limsnet.htm.

West Virginia: www.state.wv.us/taxrev/busreg.html.

Wisconsin: www.wdfi.org/corporations/forms.

Wyoming: http://soswy.state.wy.us/corporat/corporat.htm.

✔ JOIN WRITERS' ASSOCIATIONS

Trade associations for writers provide a wonderful way to network with other writers and access resources. These associations are abundant, and many have regional chapters. Most require membership dues ranging from $30 to $200. Evaluate several associations and then decide which ones fit your needs best. You may even want to join more than one.

The following are some associations to consider:

American Society of Journalists and Authors: www.asja.org.

Association of Authors and Publishers: www.authorsandpublishers.org.

Directory and Database Publishers Forum & Network: www.dpfn.com.

National Association of Women Writers: www.nationalwriters.com.

National Writers Association: www.nationalwriters.com.

PMA (Publishers Marketing Association), www.PMA-online.org.

Small Publishers, Artists, and Writers Network: www.spawn.org.

Small Publishers Association of North America: www.spannet.org.

The following are some associations with a regional focus:

Arizona Book Publishing Association: www.azbookpub.com.

Bay Area Independent Publishers Association: www.baipa.org.

Book Publishers Northwest: www.bpnw.org.

Colorado Independent Publishers Association: www.cipabooks.com.

Connecticut Authors and Publishers Association: www.aboutcapa.com.

Florida Publishers Association: www.flbookpub.org.

Illinois Women's Press Association: www.iwpa.org.

Independent Writers of Southern California: www.iwosc.org.

Minnesota Book Publishers Round Table: www.publishersroundtable.org.

New Mexico Book Association: www.nmbook.org.

Northern California Publishers & Authors: www.norcalpa.org.

Publishers Association of the South: www.pubsouth.org.

St. Louis Publishers Association: www.stlouispublishers.org.

Wisconsin Regional Writers Association: www.wrwa.net.

Writers League of Texas: www.writersleague.org.

The preceding list is just a sampling of the regional writers' trade associations. Use the Internet and a keyword search to locate additional organizations in your area. More associations are also listed at www.businessinfoguide.com/publishing.htm.

✔ ADDITIONAL BOOKS REFERENCED IN THIS TEXT

The Art of the Start: The Time-Tested, Battle-Hardened Guide for Anyone Starting Anything by Guy Kawasaki, published by Porfolio, 2004.

The Attractor Factor: 5 Easy Steps for Creating Wealth (or Anything Else) from the Inside Out by Joe Vitale, published by John Wiley & Sons, 2005.

Become the Squeaky Wheel: A Credit and Collections Guide for Everyone by Michelle Dunn, published by Never Dunn Publishing, 2005.

The Business Startup Checklist and Planning Guide: Seize Your Entrepreneurial Dreams by Stephanie Chandler, published by Aventine Press, 2005.

Chicken Soup for the Soul by Jack Canfield and Mark Victor Hansen, published by HCI, 1993.

Don't Sweat the Small Stuff . . . And It's All Small Stuff by Richard Carlson, published by Hyperion, 1997.

Good to Great: Why Some Companies Make the Leap and Others Don't by Jim Collins, published by Collins, 2001.

The Greatest Money-Making Secret in History by Joe Vitale, published by Authorhouse, 2003.

How to Buy, Sell, and Profit on eBay: Kick-Start Your Home Based Business in Just 30 Days by Adam Ginsburg, published by Collins, 2005.

Kick Start Your Success by Romanus Wolter, published by John Wiley & Sons, 2006.

Life's Missing Instruction Manual: The Guidebook You Should Have Been Given at Birth by Joe Vitale, published by John Wiley & Sons, 2006.

The Little Engine That Could by Walter Piper, published by Philomel, re-released 2005.

Making a Living without a Job: Winning Ways for Creating Work You Love by Barbara Winter, published by Bantam, 1993.

The Mars and Venus Diet and Exercise Solution by John Gray, PhD, published by HarperCollins, 1997.

Mars and Venus in the Bedroom by John Gray, PhD, published by HarperCollins, 1997.

Mars and Venus on a Date by John Gray, PhD, Published by HarperCollins, 1997.

Men Are from Mars, Women Are from Venus by John Gray, PhD, published by HarperCollins, 1993.

Million Dollar Consulting by Alan Weiss, published by McGraw-Hill, 2002, 3rd edition.

Patent It Yourself by David Pressman, published by NOLO, 2005, 11th edition.

Principled Profit: Marketing That Puts People First by Shel Horowitz, published by Accurate Writing and More, 2003.

Sell Yourself without Selling Your Soul: A Woman's Guide to Promoting Herself, Her Business, Her Product, or Her Cause with Integrity and Spirit by Susan Harrow, published by HarperCollins, 2003.

The Seven Lost Secrets of Success by Joe Vitale, published by Morgan James Publishing, 2005.

Starting a Collections Agency by Michelle Dunn, published by Mad Collection Agency, 2000.

Starting an Online Business for Dummies by Greg Holden, published by For Dummies, 2005, 4th edition.

There's a Customer Born Every Minute: P. T. Barnum's Amazing 10 Rings of Power for Creating Fame, Fortune, and a Business Empire Today—Guaranteed by Joe Vitale, published by John Wiley & Sons, 2006, revised edition.

The Ultimate Guide to Electronic Marketing for Small Business: Low Cost/High Return Tools and Techniques That Really Work by Tom Antion, published by John Wiley & Sons, 2005.

The White Paper Marketing Handbook by Robert W. Bly, published by South-Western Educational Publishing, 2006.

INDEX

About the Author

Stephanie Chandler is the founder of BusinessInfoGuide.com, a directory of free resources for entrepreneurs, and the owner of Book Lovers Bookstore in Sacramento, California. She is also a professionally trained public speaker, has published articles in a variety of magazines and newspapers, and is the author of *The Business Startup Checklist and Planning Guide: Seize Your Entrepreneurial Dreams!* (Aventine Press, September 2005).

After developing an ulcer before her thirtieth birthday, Chandler knew it was time for a complete lifestyle change. She kissed off corporate America in 2003 to pursue her entrepreneurial dreams and has never looked back. She resides in Northern California with her husband (a patient man who makes her laugh every day), stepson, a one-eyed cat, and an intellectually challenged rescue-mutt named Mojo. At the time this book went to press, she also became a new mom to a beautiful son named Benjamin.

Visit Stephanie Chandler's web sites:

- ✔ www.businessinfoguide.com
- ✔ www.stephaniechandler.com
- ✔ www.bookloverscafe.com